Improving STUDENT LEARNING

A Strategic Plan for Education Research and Its Utilization

Committee on a Feasibility Study for a
Strategic Education Research Program

Commission on Behavioral and
Social Sciences and Education

National Research Council

NATIONAL ACADEMY PRESS
Washington, DC

NATIONAL ACADEMY PRESS
2101 Constitution Avenue, NW • Washington, DC   20418

NOTICE: The project that is the subject of this report was approved by the Governing Board of the National Research Council, whose members are drawn from the councils of the National Academy of Sciences, the National Academy of Engineering, and the Institute of Medicine. The members of the committee responsible for the report were chosen for their special competences and with regard for appropriate balance.

This study was supported by the National Research Council.

Library of Congress Cataloging-in-Publication Data

Improving student learning : a strategic plan for education
research and its utilization / Committee on a Feasibility Study for
a Strategic Education Research Program, Commission on Behavioral
and Social Sciences and Education, National Research Council.
     p. cm.
    Includes bibliographical references.
    ISBN 0-309-06489-9 (pbk.)
    1. Education—Research—United States. 2. School improvement
programs—United States. I. National Research Council (U.S.).
Committee on a Feasibility Study for a Strategic Education
Research Program.
    LB1028.25.U6I66 1999
    370'.7'20973—dc21

                                   99-6599

Additional copies of this report are available from:

National Academy Press
2101 Constitution Avenue, N.W.
Lock Box 285
Washington, D.C. 20055
Call 800-624-6242 or 202-334-3313 (in the Washington Metropolitan Area).

This report is also available on line at **http://www.nap.edu**

Printed in the United States of America

The National Academy of Sciences is a private, nonprofit, self-perpetuating society of distinguished scholars engaged in scientific and engineering research, dedicated to the furtherance of science and technology and to their use for the general welfare. Upon the authority of the charter granted to it by the Congress in 1863, the Academy has a mandate that requires it to advise the federal government on scientific and technical matters. Dr. Bruce M. Alberts is president of the National Academy of Sciences.

The National Academy of Engineering was established in 1964, under the charter of the National Academy of Sciences, as a parallel organization of outstanding engineers. It is autonomous in its administration and in the selection of its members, sharing with the National Academy of Sciences the responsibility for advising the federal government. The National Academy of Engineering also sponsors engineering programs aimed at meeting national needs, encourages education and research, and recognizes the superior achievements of engineers. Dr. William A. Wulf is president of the National Academy of Engineering.

The Institute of Medicine was established in 1970 by the National Academy of Sciences to secure the services of eminent members of appropriate professions in the examination of policy matters pertaining to the health of the public. The Institute acts under the responsibility given to the National Academy of Sciences by its congressional charter to be an adviser to the federal government and, upon its own initiative, to identify issues of medical care, research, and education. Dr. Kenneth I. Shine is president of the Institute of Medicine.

The National Research Council was organized by the National Academy of Sciences in 1916 to associate the broad community of science and technology with the Academy's purposes of furthering knowledge and advising the federal government. Functioning in accordance with general policies determined by the Academy, the Council has become the principal operating agency of both the National Academy of Sciences and the National Academy of Engineering in providing services to the government, the public, and the scientific and engineering communities. The Council is administered jointly by both Academies and the Institute of Medicine. Dr. Bruce M. Alberts and Dr. William A. Wulf are chairman and vice chairman, respectively, of the National Research Council.

Contents

3   Getting Answers: Designing a Strategic Research Program   49

References   67

Preface

I t has been my good fortune to chair the National Research Council (NRC) for the last 6 years. The NRC is the operating arm of the National Academy of Sciences, the National Academy of Engineering, and the Institute of Medicine—four nongovernmental organizations that are collectively referred to as the National Academies. The NRC focuses on harnessing the best science in order to improve the general welfare. At the request of the government, we carry out studies that cover an enormous variety of important issues— biodiversity, global warming, human nutritional requirements, health and behavior, and human learning to name a few. Many thousands of the nation's leading scientists, engineers, medical experts, policy experts, and practitioners contribute their time and knowledge to these projects every year. In nearly every study we do, we are building new collaborations across disciplines and professions, so as to bring the best resources to bear on important problems.

Over the last decade, education has become a central element in the NRC program. In 1996, we completed a 4-year project to develop national standards for science education in the primary and secondary grades. Hundreds of scientists and educators were involved in developing these standards, and the draft standards were sent to 40,000 people for comment. At about the same time, we established a new Center for Science, Mathematics, and Engineering Education. In addition, our Commission on Behavioral and Social Sciences and Education has undertaken many important studies on issues in testing and assessment, education finance, preventing reading difficulties in young children, and human learning and educational practice.

As I survey the work of the National Research Council, it is poignantly clear that research has not had the kind of impact on education that is visible in medical practice, space exploration, energy, and many other fields. My personal experience as a scientist who worked to improve science instruction in the San Francisco public elementary schools in the 1980s and early 1990s gave me a sense of how difficult and complicated it is to reform education. Over the past 6 years of my presidency, my conversations with educators, reform leaders, and researchers in virtually every part of the country have convinced me that even the most successful innovations will fail to take root and spread—unless the reform dynamic changes substantially.

This small book has a very big ambition: to increase the usefulness and relevance of research to educational practice. The report outlines a highly focused program of research designed to support improved student learning, proposing a new model—drawn in part from the MacArthur Foundation research networks—for carrying out that research. Most significantly, this Strategic Education Research Program (SERP) calls for a new kind of collaboration that will respect and involve not only the many scientific disciplines that have something to contribute to education, but also those individuals who understand education from the inside: teachers, administrators, and policy makers.

The idea for this Strategic Education Research Program came from a very unlikely source: highway research. In the 1980s, highway research had very little impact on the construction and repair of the nation's highways and roads. The research that was done was disconnected from the needs of the practitioners—those who build highways. As a result, state agencies saw each dollar spent on research as one dollar less for badly needed construction, as did the construction industry. And yet the nation's roads were poorly built. The NRC undertook a study to see if the disparate interests could unite to support a research agenda of great practical importance. As a consequence of that study, Congress enacted a 10-year, $150 million Strategic Highway Research Program (SHRP) in 1985. The SHRP was administered by the NRC's Transportation Research Board, and it brought the research, policy, and practice communities together in a concerted effort that all could support. By the time it ended, SHRP had not only produced results that were widely recognized as useful, it had also created stronger links among the research, policy, and practice communities.

What do U.S. highways and education have in common? Both are administered by the states. Both involve a large public investment. Both badly need research that speaks to the needs of everyday practice. There are obvious limits to the analogy, but the success of SHRP led us to wonder if a similar effort could propel a widespread process of education reform. The presidents of the National Academies underwrote this project to explore the feasibility of mounting a strategic program of research in education. I joined the group of educators, policy experts, and researchers who undertook the study at many of their meetings. We think we have a powerful idea and at least the beginnings of a plan.

But such a large research effort and the new kinds of collaborations it will require are unlikely to spring fully formed from the work of one committee. It is now time to engage in a larger conversation among educators, policy makers, and researchers—as well as with the public- and private-sector organizations that are the SERP's likely sponsors. On behalf of the National Academies, I invite all interested parties to join in a year of public dialogue concerning a Strategic Education Research Program. How can we best work together to build a science of education that optimizes the potential of students, teachers, and schools—creating a practice of education that continually improves as it incorporates the best available knowledge about learning and teaching for all kinds of children? Knowing that there is no more important question for the future of our nation, I hope that this report will catalyze new partnerships and major new investments in education to provide the badly needed answers.

Bruce Alberts
President, National Academy of Sciences
Chair, National Research Council

Acknowledgments

This report has been reviewed in draft form by individuals chosen for their diverse perspectives and technical expertise, in accordance with procedures approved by the Report Review Committee of the National Research Council. The purpose of this independent review is to provide candid and critical comments that will assist the institution in making the published report as sound as possible and to ensure that the report meets institutional standards for objectivity, evidence, and responsiveness to the study charge. The review comments and draft manuscript remain confidential to protect the integrity of the deliberative process.

We thank the following individuals for their participation in the review of this report: Christopher Cross, Council for Basic Education, Washington, D.C.; Jay W. Forrester, Sloan School of Management, Massachusetts Institute of Technology; Timothy H. Goldsmith, Department of Biology, Yale University; Paul Goren, John D. and Catherine T. MacArthur Foundation, Chicago, Ill.; Donald Kennedy, Institute for International Studies, Stanford University; Michael W. Kirst, School of Education, Stanford University; Gardner Lindzey, Center for Advanced Study in the Behavioral Sciences, Stanford, Calif.; Lorraine McDonnell, Department of Political Science, University of California, Santa Barbara; and William Morrill, Mathtech, Inc., Princeton, N.J.

Although the individuals listed above have provided constructive comments and suggestions, it must be emphasized that responsibility for the final content of this report rests entirely with the authoring committee and the institution.

Improving STUDENT LEARNING

Executive Summary

ducation in the United States currently consumes about 7 percent of the gross domestic product, yet the state of education is increasingly an issue of deep concern to parents, political leaders, employers, and the public generally. The recognition that many big-city schools, particularly the schools that serve poor children, have become failures for almost all students has given particular urgency to the issue of school reform. As *Education Week* (1998:6) put it recently, "It's hard to exaggerate the education crisis in America's cities."

One striking fact is that the complex world of education—unlike defense, health care, or industrial production—does not rest on a strong research base. In no other field are personal experience and ideology so frequently relied on to make policy choices, and in no other field is the research base so inadequate and little used. Comparatively little research is funded, and the task of importing even the strongest research findings into over a million classrooms is daunting.

In 1996 the National Research Council, the operating arm of the National Academy of Sciences and the National Academy of Engineering (henceforth, the Academies), launched a study to determine the feasibility of mounting a long-term, strategic program of research focused on a limited number of topics judged to be of crucial importance for improving student learning in the nation's schools. The study was conducted by a multi-disciplinary committee composed of education researchers, practitioners, policy makers and other experts chosen to bring the widest possible range of perspectives to this task.

FOUR KEY QUESTIONS

The result of the committee's deliberations is a proposal for an ambitious and extraordinary experiment: the establishment of a Strategic Education Research Program (SERP) that would focus the energies of a significant number of researchers, practitioners, and policy makers on obtaining the answers to four specific, interrelated questions. The first three questions address fundamental issues in education:

• **How can advances in research on human cognition, development, and learning be incorporated into educational practice?**
• **How can student engagement in the learning process and motivation to achieve in school be increased?**
• **How can schools and school districts be transformed into organizations that have the capacity to continuously improve their practices?**

The committee selected these three questions for a number of reasons. Together they lie at the heart of education. It is possible, in seeking answers to them, to draw on substantial research as well as to imagine the outlines of future studies. They speak directly to the problems that teachers and school officials encounter and to the concerns of parents and the public more generally. Perhaps most important, they hold the potential for leveraging large improvements in student performance.

How to realize this potential is not self-evident. There is no doubt that educational practice can be strengthened by careful scientific research. But it is not clear how to make the integration of research findings an organic part of the education system. Therefore, the committee proposes a fourth and overarching research question:

• **How can the use of research knowledge be increased in schools and school districts?**

This question, expressed variously as knowledge utilization or knowledge mobilization, raises issues about the preparation of teachers so that they can be consumers of research, about the

There is no doubt that educational practice can be strengthened by careful scientific research design of schools to create effective learning environments, and about bringing policy into alignment with new strategies for teaching and learning. Above all, however, it is about the *translation* of research findings into forms useful for educational practice. It will require large-scale, systematic experimentation and demonstration to transform knowledge about human learning and the development of competence into the working vocabulary of teachers and schools.

• •

THE PROPOSED STRATEGIC EDUCATION RESEARCH PROGRAM

To address these questions, the committee calls for a large-scale and sharply defined program of research, demonstration, and evaluation. Much of the work will need to be embedded in school settings; all of it should be informed by the needs of the most challenging schools, in particular, high-poverty urban schools. The likelihood of real accomplishment will be increased to the extent that a process of continuous incorporation of findings is used to create a flexible design for the array of SERP investigations.

> Much of the work
> will need to be
> embedded in
> school settings

To initiate and guide these activities, the committee proposes the establishment of four interconnected networks:

- a learning and instruction network,
- a student motivation network,
- a transforming schools network, and
- a utilization network.

Each network will include distinguished researchers working in partnership with practitioners and policy makers and supported by a national coalition of public and private funding organizations and other stakeholders, including legislators, state education agencies, teacher associations, organizations representing the research community, and other groups. Members of the four SERP networks would conduct research designed to help answer each network's hub question. They would also stimulate other researchers to undertake relevant studies, synthesize findings from their own and others' work, and plan future investigations. In addition, a major preoccupation of all four networks, but especially the fourth, would be to find ways to ensure utilization of the research by practitioners. A core premise of the plan is that the program of research, synthesis, and implementation activities will be strengthened by the interactions among researchers, practitioners, and policy makers in the networks.

Given the complexity of the issues, the magnitude of the research challenge, and the stakes involved, the committee strongly recommends that this program be implemented with the expectation that it will continue for at least 15 years. The committee is confident, however, that significant contributions to educational systems will be possible within the first 5-7 years because a considerable body of potentially useful research already exists in each area.

The committee offers suggestions for organization and management of the overall program in the body of this report. The suggestions do not add up to a blueprint for SERP; a detailed plan can only emerge through discussions among all the professional groups in education and the potential funders of the program—federal, state, and private. But we are proposing a new model for education research as the heart of the SERP idea. This new model has six of the crucial features: (1) promotion of collaborative and interdisciplinary work; (2) provision of constant, ongoing commitment on the part of core teams of researchers; (3) a built-in partnership with the practice and policy communities; (4) iterative and interactive interplay between basic and applied research in a structure that combines the richness of field-initiated research and the purpose of program-driven research; (5) a plan that is sustained over a long enough time for results to be cumulative; and (6) an overall structure that is cumulative in nature—each step planned to build on previous steps.

Our excitement about the idea of a Strategic Education Research Program has not blinded us to the risks. It is clear that the quality of both scientific and organizational leadership will determine its success. The intellectual and management challenges that will have to be met are formidable and will demand exceptional talent, commitment, and perseverance on the part of all of those responsible for it.

This new model [for education research] has . . . a built-in partnership with the practice and policy communities

How This Plan Differs from Other Efforts

Many individuals and organizations have recognized the potential importance of research to education. There have been numerous university-based and district-based efforts to narrow the gap between research and practice. At the national level, the U.S. Department of Education and the National Educational Research Policy and Priorities Board have constructed a broad framework for education research, identifying seven broad challenges that warrant public investment. All these efforts continue to make important contributions to the nation's education, but they do not rigorously focus the nation's knowledge, resources, and energies in order to improve student learning. They do not promote the systematic use of research by teachers, administrators, and policy officials to improve student achievement. And because political priorities tend to change frequently, they tend not to produce sustained and cumulating knowledge.

The Strategic Education Research Program proposed in this document represents the first large-scale effort of its kind. By design, the SERP plan is focused, collaborative, cumulative, sustained, and solutions oriented.

By design, the SERP plan is focused, collaborative, cumulative, sustained, and solutions oriented

- *Focused* SERP targets four hub research questions that hold great promise for strengthening learning in U.S. schools. This strategic focus will help harness the nation's powerful intellectual resources and expertise, making the networks more productive, more closely linked to classroom practice, and more accountable for demonstrable progress.
- *Collaborative* Finding answers to each of the hub research questions will require the combined insights of many fields—including cognitive functioning, social processes, and organizational change—as well as the deployment of the full array of research methods. Asking the right questions will require the wisdom of those who are deeply engaged in practice and the insights of policy makers. The organization of the effort through carefully coordinated networks of researchers, educators, and policy experts will promote the needed cross-fertilization that is commonly missing from current research efforts.
- *Cumulative* SERP recognizes that the traditional linear model of research—from basic research to applications—has not been productive in changing complex social systems like

education. It envisions a new model of research, combining elements of field-initiated and program-driven research within a structure that will encourage a continuous process of taking stock so that each stage builds on what has been learned. Research or demonstrations in applied settings are as likely to define the next basic research questions as vice versa.

• *Sustained* SERP will function over a 15-year period (with decision points about continuation along the way), with constant, ongoing commitment on the part of its participants. Network members will maintain their own identities and activities in their particular professions and disciplines, but they will commit a substantial portion of their time and effort to network activities for more than a decade.

• *Solutions Oriented* SERP involves practitioners and policy makers in helping to define problems, devise solutions, and monitor the effects of research-based approaches. This built-in partnership with the policy and practice communities should have the healthy side-effect of cultivating a greater readiness on the part of local communities and schools to view research as a source of solutions for educational problems.

How This Plan Relates to Other Efforts

For the SERP idea to come to fruition, education leaders will need to see its potential for leveraging existing investments by federal and state governments, school systems, and private-sector organizations. The idea is not to replace important research and reform programs, but to strengthen them by finding unrealized synergies, providing a powerful focus for the related activities, synthesizing what is known, and filling in gaps in the research. SERP could, for example, become a conduit for synthesizing and transmitting the findings from research, development, and demonstration projects supported by the Department of Education through its regional laboratories and research and development (R&D) centers; by the National Science Foundation through its cognitive research program, its new technology and learning centers, its Statewide Systemic Initiative (SSI); and by the National Institute for Child Health and Human Development, which has a strong program of research on the mechanisms of cognition and learning. SERP could also support the translation of research findings into practice by linking up with or supporting demonstration projects.

Not least, it would support fledgling efforts to build better bridges, based on a foundation of mutual respect, between the practitioner and the research communities.

WHY A STRATEGIC PLAN IS NEEDED

In part, the need for a strategic research plan grows out of the highly decentralized organization of education in the United States. More concretely, the answer lies with American students and American schools. Many students perform at high levels, but the nation's continued vitality as a democracy and its productivity in a global economy will hinge in coming decades on the knowledge and skills of the majority—the tens of millions of children who are not realizing their full capacities and are therefore unable to meet the intellectual demands of modern life and work.

Imagine what could be accomplished if the nation committed itself to a concerted effort to find out what needs to be known in order to improve achievement among *these* children. Imagine what they might achieve if the nation's leading researchers and education experts were to concentrate—not just for a month or a year, but for more than a decade—on how to facilitate and motivate *their* learning. That is the mission of the strategic plan for education research and its utilization presented in this report.

More concretely,

the answer lies with

American students

and American

schools

NEXT STEPS

In the Preface, Bruce Alberts expresses his hope that this report will catalyze major new investments in education. As a first step, the National Academies propose to launch a year-long national dialogue during which the idea for a Strategic Education Research Program is discussed with all of the professional groups involved in education.

This committee strongly endorses that plan: We urge the federal government—in particular, the Department of Education and the National Science Foundation—major foundations whose mission includes improving education, state and local education leaders, and education research organizations to join the Academies in this year of dialogue to see if, together, we can transform the SERP idea into a productive collaboration to use the power of science to improve education in the United States.

1 Can Research Serve the Needs of Education?

This report presents the general outlines for a program of research designed to strengthen current efforts for education reform. It advances a strategy to focus education research on a few critical topics that both address needs identified in professional practice and are likely to produce large payoffs. The committee hopes that the report will, at the very least, generate interest and stimulate discussion about how to use the power of scientific research to improve education. It is an invitation to everyone involved in education to discuss the feasibility of the proposed plan, to work out the details, perhaps to become allies in a common cause.

The report is thus addressed to many audiences. It is addressed to the federal government—federal dollars now constitute between 60 and 75 percent of total national resources for education research. It is addressed to state and local officials who have primary responsibility for the American education system. It is addressed to the thousands of teachers and administrators who every day face the immediate realities of educating America's children. It is addressed to the community of scientists and scholars who command powerful tools of analysis and observation that could strengthen teaching and learning. And finally, it is addressed to the philanthropic organizations that have played such an important role in promoting education during the course of this century.

EDUCATION REFORM AND EDUCATION RESEARCH

EDUCATION REFORM: AN AMERICAN PASSION

Since the time of the Revolution, education has been an important part of the American ethos. When Europeans claimed that the social fabric would disintegrate without a king, the founders of the Republic argued that an educated citizenry would hold the polity together. A century later, as waves of newcomers filled the land, schooling was promoted as the way to make them Americans, to knit together a nation of immigrants. Now, two centuries later, the United States is in the midst of fundamental transitions: it can no longer dominate the world politically or economically as it did in the 35 years after World War II; industrial production is migrating overseas, changing the nature—and the intellectual and technical demands—of the contemporary workplace; the concentration of poverty and disadvantage that characterizes large cities has become an intransigent problem. Once again, education is at the top of the national political agenda. Every state has mandated reforms and countless local programs and alliances have initiated efforts for improvements.

Because education holds so central a place in the nation, education reform efforts in the United States have been almost continuous. These efforts have been based on passion, conviction, and, occasionally, research. Almost all have been declared a success by at least some people. And indisputable progress has been made in terms of school attendance, years of schooling, levels of literacy, and the quality of classrooms and equipment. Yet, as the twentieth century ends, few people are fully satisfied with the condition of education in the United States

Many individuals and institutions have been involved in school reform. From the great education reformers of the nineteenth century—Horace Mann in the 1840s, John Dewey in the 1890s—to the major philanthropies in the twentieth century—the Carnegie, Spencer, and Ford Foundations and the Julius Rosenwald Fund (which built schools all over the South) the idea of improving education in order to improve society has been a powerful force. Since the 1850s, when the principle of

> Education reform
>
> efforts in the
>
> United States
>
> have been almost
>
> continuous

state-supported schools for all children triumphed in most parts of the country, state and local governments have played a central role in the governance of what rapidly became "school systems." In successive waves of reformist sentiment, schools have been used as the instrument for shaping a rural populace into an increasingly urban and industrial one.

Each reform attempt is an exercise in optimism and creativity. Reform efforts require considerable energy and commitment. They also require financial resources and long time horizons. The dynamism and ferment that characterize education reform efforts in the United States have led to significant change and progress on many fronts. But the country has undergone even greater change, with the consequence that public frustration with the quality of education in the United States has been as constant as reform efforts.

Can the balance between optimism and frustration be shifted? Can the likelihood that reform efforts will produce students who are better learners be increased?

Each reform
attempt is an
exercise in
optimism and
creativity

THE ROLE OF RESEARCH[1]

Research is one of the most important tools society has for ensuring that government policies and practices are thoughtful and effective. Research has, for example, been a potent force for improved public health: because of advances in biomedical research that produced the polio vaccine, public health officials could confidently inoculate the entire youth population with a live virus. So axiomatic is the profitability of research in agriculture that one of the nation's foremost seed companies was willing to invest 40 years of effort in the development of a seedless watermelon.

In education, however, the potential of research has not been realized. The sheer complexity of the enterprise has been a factor, as have underinvestment, lack of focus, and the difficulties of translating research results for practical ends.

---

[1]This section draws on an earlier report, *Research and Education Reform: Roles for the Office of Educational Research and Improvement* (National Research Council, 1992).

Complexity

Education in the United States is an extraordinarily complex, dynamic system, which has to continually adapt to changes in the society. More centralized systems or more traditional societies, or simply smaller countries, present more manageable challenges for designing education research, but in any setting it must deal with the behavior and development of individual students, group dynamics of the classroom, and institutional change of school systems—all in the context of the evolving needs of the society. Research in education examines an ever-changing process, without end and without final answers. Yet good research can often make the difference between adaptations that improve the educational process and those that don't.

Underinvestment

The federal government has made major investments in research in many fields in the last half century. As a result, medical treatment, defense, agriculture, space exploration, technology, and other social goods have made important progress. Although between 60 and 75 percent of support for education research comes from the federal government; that represents less than 1 percent of federal spending on education. And the dollar amount pales when compared with federal support of medical, defense, or even agricultural research. From another view, although education for kindergarten through grade 12 (K-12) costs close to $340 billion per year (U.S. Department of Education, 1997), virtually no state funding supports education research. In short, the nation has made an enormous social investment in education with relatively little reflection, scientific rigor, or quality control.

Lack of Focus

Past investments in education research can only be described as diffuse. K-12 schooling in the United States is such a vast enterprise and takes place in such diverse settings that letting "a thousand flowers bloom" in education research appeared to

Research in education examines an ever-changing process

be a sensible, responsive approach. The federal bodies that set priorities for education research have tended to frame their agendas very broadly. The foundations and agencies that fund research have encouraged and supported an extremely wide spectrum of research and development activities. This approach has resulted in innovative studies, fascinating findings, and isolated success stories, but it has not had the widespread effects on student learning that would create demand for the fruits of research. The National Research Council's recent assessment of the federal role in supporting education research concluded that the agencies responsible for education research have spread their limited resources "so thinly that mediocrity was almost assured. Only a few lines of research have been sustained for the time needed to bring them to fruition" (National Research Council, 1992:3).

Difficulties of Translating Research

Because educational practice in the United States is controlled at the local, indeed, the classroom level, the challenge of incorporating even the strongest research findings into over a million classrooms is daunting. It is not that most people who are involved in helping children learn do not want to do a better job. Parents and teachers want their children to succeed. Policy makers and administrators want to improve the performance of their schools. Curriculum developers and entrepreneurs want to develop new ideas and provide new products. But few of these people have access to research findings, and there is no centralized system (such as exists in Japan or France) to convey the most important research knowledge and to systematically train practitioners in its application. Furthermore, the language of researchers is not the language of practitioners; there is a cultural divide that hampers accessibility, and the incentive structures in research universities tend not to reward researcher-practitioner interface. As a consequence, improvement efforts, no matter how conscientious or well intentioned, are—and are likely to remain—hit-or-miss attempts.

Parents and teachers want their children to succeed

TOWARD A STRATEGIC APPROACH TO RESEARCH

The challenge

of incorporating

. . . research

findings into

over a million

classrooms is

daunting

Despite this picture of unfilled promise, the nation does have resources to strengthen the role of research in education. Education researchers have at their disposal some very powerful scientific tools and access to a broad research literature in the behavioral, cognitive, and social sciences. For their part, teachers know the problems of education at first hand; like anthropologists, they understand the texture and rhythms of school life and learning, and many have crafted local solutions to difficult problems. Policy makers understand the larger realities of education—bureaucratic inertia, the difficulties of system-wide change, the political and economic dimensions of education. Can these considerable resources and energies be concentrated on the task of increasing the usefulness of research for policy makers, administrators, teachers, and others who have responsibility for the nation's schools?

To explore this challenge, in 1996 the National Research Council, the working arm of the National Academy of Sciences, convened a committee of 16 people broadly representative of the target communities: researchers in various fields, teachers, state- and district-level administrators, policy makers with federal and state experience, and analysts who have watched and commented on the education enterprise from some remove. The committee was asked to address four questions:

- Is it possible to identify a limited set of research questions of such crucial importance that answers to them could strengthen schools and bring about substantial improvement in student learning?
- Can a group of leading researchers, policy makers, and practitioners agree on what those questions would be?
- What would it take—in terms of resources, time, and organizational capacity—to answer those questions?
- What would it take to ensure the utilization of knowledge and solutions emerging from this effort?

The committee grappled with these questions over a 2-year period. Its members took a hard look at the field of education research, assessing the strengths and weaknesses of the existing knowledge base. They came back again and again to the real problems that teachers and principles and superintendents face every day and to the special needs of schools and students in communities plagued by poverty and its attendant problems.

The committee also discussed at length what a *strategic* research program would look like. The committee became convinced that a Strategic Education Research Program as proposed in the following pages could increase the potential of research to improve education by focusing attention and resources on a limited number of critically important research questions and by placing utilization issues at the core of the effort.

DEFINING STRATEGIC

While "strategic" is easy to understand in games like chess and in a military context (e.g., destroying industrial plants and communications facilities to compromise an opponent's capacity to mount military operations), what does it mean in the more pacific realms of learning and education? Having in mind one clear and overriding goal—substantially improving students' learning—the committee ultimately identified seven characteristics that would make a program of education research strategic.

• **Strategic research would both advance fundamental scientific understanding and serve practical needs.**[2] If administrators, teachers, and other educators are to become consumers of research, then the research community will have to pay far closer attention to the needs of practitioners and policy makers. Conversely, if the ultimate goal of education reform is to improve all student learning and not just in a few classes or schools, then reformers would do well to build on systematic knowledge and the scientific tradition of hypothesis testing. Scientific knowledge about the workings of the mind and the

------

[2]For an interesting discussion of the need to move beyond artificial distinctions between basic and applied science, see Stokes (1997).

brain or the processes of learning, for example, can and should inform reform efforts.

• **Strategic research would be highly focused.** Improving student learning requires substantial resources and public resolve; supplies of both tend to be limited. It is therefore necessary to focus on a few very high priorities.

• **Strategic research would address topics of self-evident importance.** To be strategic, research must address topics that parents and the general public believe are crucial to improving the quality of education. Each topic should be grounded in the concerns of policy makers, teachers, administrators, and researchers, and solutions to each problem should be seen as valuable from all of their perspectives.

• **Strategic research would be high-leverage research.** The goal, in other words, is to pick topics likely to have the most effect on the specified outcome—in this case, improved student learning.

• **Strategic research would address issues that form a coherent set.** Focusing strategically suggests that each topic should be relevant to the others so that results are mutually reinforcing. This internal coherence will increase the likelihood that the institutions and individuals who influence children's learning will see the benefit of using well-tested education research.

• **Strategic research would be located at the nexus of scientific opportunity and practical need.** It is critically important that the selected research topics are the product of informed estimates of scientific promise and likely to engage the most able researchers so that there is reason to believe that the program can be successful. At the same time, the research topics need to reflect issues and problems that are important to teachers, administrators, and policy makers.

And, finally:

• **Strategic education research requires continuity.** As with other complex social systems, the problems and inadequacies in education defy simple solutions or magic bullets. In addition to focus and leverage and the other characteristics described above, it will require sustained attention over time to build a strong body of research that is useful—and used—in education.

A strategic

plan, by

definition,

has focus

and

coherence

BENEFITS OF A STRATEGIC PLAN

In considering what strategic means in the context of education research, the committee also considered the benefits of such a program in comparison with the more scattershot approach that has typified education improvement and research. A strategic plan, by definition, has focus and coherence. Existing school improvement efforts are fragmented and largely uninformed by research. To have researchers, policy makers, and practitioners focus on a compelling set of educational issues and to conduct, disseminate, and apply research that addresses those issues could be a powerful engine for change.

At the same time, a successful Strategic Education Research Program (SERP) of the kind proposed would seek to create a durable structure linking researchers, policy makers, and practitioners. The plan presented in this report provides for ongoing contacts among these actors and tries to ensure that knowledge and expertise move in all directions. In particular, it positions teachers both to help define the focus of research and to become active consumers of education research.

A strategic program could also draw public attention to the utility of education research. Research and its dissemination are often a "hard sell" because they strike taxpayers as remote from their most urgent concern—improving student learning. A large-scale, strategic plan for improving student learning through research and knowledge would send a strong message that research and knowledge matter in the realm of education—that can and do translate into achievement gains for children.

HOW THIS PLAN RELATES TO OTHER EFFORTS

While the SERP we propose is different from other reform efforts, it is emphatically not a replacement for them. For the SERP idea to come to life, education leaders will have to see its potential as a vehicle for leveraging existing investments by the federal government, state governments, school systems, and private-sector organizations. The U.S. Department of Education, the National Science Foundation (NSF), the National Institute of Child Health and Human Development (NICHD), the Office of Naval Research (ONR), to name a few players at the federal level, have important ongoing programs supporting research and reform efforts. We believe a strategic research program can strengthen them and help them realize their goals.

The Department of Education's Office of Education Research and Improvement (OERI) supports 12 research and development (R&D) centers and 10 regional laboratories. Established in the mid-1960s in response to concerns about the quality of education, the OERI centers have engaged in a shifting menu of basic and applied research and development. Several have made outstanding contributions over the years: the Learning Research and Development Center at the University of Pittsburgh, formerly an OERI center, has been a leader in the application of cognitive science to education; the Center for Research on Evaluation, Standards, and Student Testing at the University of California at Los Angeles, a current one, has had a positive influence on testing research and policy. But with modest federal funds divided among many centers (each receiving approximately $1 million per year over a 5-year grant cycle) and each center pursuing its own mission, the centers do not represent the "critical mass" needed for significant progress in a major, complex field.

In contrast to the R&D centers, the OERI regional laboratories have focused primarily on demonstrations, the development and dissemination of materials to state and local educational officials and technical assistance to educators. The 10 labs have focused on bridging the gap between research and practice. In general, surveys of educators suggest that the dissemination activities of the regional labs are reaching their audience. But evaluations of the labs have found little communication and coordination among the regional labs and the centers, although there are a few notable exceptions (Cross, 1989; Turnbull et al., 1994).

In a somewhat different vein, in 1991 the National Science Foundation began an ambitious Statewide Systemic Initiative (SSI)—later expanded to include more focused urban and rural initiatives—to try to combat the overwhelming tendency of education reforms to be swallowed up by the existing system. The SSI is built on a set of ideas, articulated powerfully by Marshall Smith and Jennifer O'Day (Smith and O'Day, 1991; O'Day and Smith, 1993), that focus on the need for coherence and alignment of all parts of the education system. Some 26 states (including Puerto Rico) and 22 cities have received grants to date, and each was encouraged to develop its own vision of reform of science and mathematics education. Although none of the initiatives has been adopted on a statewide basis and there have been some outright failures, many of the participants think the SSI has been a worthwhile experiment. No one would claim that 7 years and an expenditure of $600 million has transformed science and mathematics education in any of the participating states or cities (Mervis, 1998). But much has been learned and even more will be learned as evaluations and case studies accumulate.

A very different approach to education reform is proposed in the so-called PCAST report, *The Use of Technology to Strengthen K-12 Education in the United States* (President's Committee of Advisors on Science and Technology, 1997). This wide-ranging proposal calls for a very sizable investment in research on the use of technology to enhance learning. It touches on many important issues, including curriculum content and pedagogy, professional development, and equitable access to technology. It recommends a major program of experimental research— basic research in learning-related disciplines such as cognitive science and developmental psychology, early-stage research on the implementation of theory-based instructional programs, large-scale empirical studies to identify effective approaches to the use of technology in education. This proposal has not yet been implemented, but its lack of reference to any of the other major reform efforts suggests that its coordination with other current efforts may be modest.

It is possible to glimpse bigger possibilities in these programs—important research findings, helpful dissemination activities, valuable experience in making the many components of school systems work more effectively together, and the goal of making computer technology a useful tool in education—a whole that is something more than the sum of its parts. One could go on to the myriad of state and local reform efforts, foundation activities, and popular school improvement campaigns. The picture of current activities that emerges is a potpourri of programs and activities that together represent an enormous expenditure of energy and political capital but that exhibit an equally striking lack of coordination. The OERI centers are, for the most part, on too small a scale to make a difference. The regional labs are supposed to bridge the gap between research and practice, but they are only modestly coordinated with the centers. Moreover, the very distinctions

What we do

have is an idea

for a vehicle . . .

that until now has

been lacking

between the missions of research centers and practitioner-oriented labs are likely to be a bar to the effectiveness of the OERI program. The National Science Foundation, in leaving the design of the SSI to each grantee, was not in a position to infuse the program with the cognitive and learning research it has supported over the years nor to build on the work of its sister agencies, the Department of Education and NICHD. To the extent that they exist, outside evaluations of the current programs suggest that, while each has been able to accomplish useful things, none has fulfilled its potential. The PCAST proposal may also represent the same danger—reasonable but too uncoordinated and too small to make a real difference in the nation's education systems.

Can the energy, the creativity, the insights, and the lessons learned from the many research programs and reform efforts be more effectively focused? We do not claim to have the blueprint in hand for accomplishing this task. What we do have is an idea for a vehicle, a program of use-inspired research that is strategic enough to reinforce and extend what is good in current research and reform efforts and to create a synergy among the organizations—federal, state, and private—that until now has been lacking.

The next two chapters lay out the elements of that idea: a strategic plan for education research and its utilization.

2 Focusing Our Efforts: Four Key Questions

A t the heart of the committee's deliberations was the issue of focus: Could the 16 members, drawn from very different parts of the education enterprise, reach agreement on a limited number of questions around which to build a large-scale research program? The early views of committee members ranged from agnostic to skeptical. The group considered a wide range of research topics, searching for those with the greatest potential for improving student learning. Over time, various members made compelling cases for specific lines of research. As the discussion matured, so did the selection criteria.

In setting its priorities, the committee asked, "Which questions, had we answers to them, would make a significant difference in student learning?" After extensive debate, the committee reached consensus on four key questions that warrant intensive, focused research efforts. These topics are presented as questions from the perspective of the school.

- **How can advances in research on human cognition, development, and learning be incorporated into educational practice?**
- **How can student engagement in the learning process and motivation to achieve in school be increased?**
- **How can schools and school districts be transformed into organizations that have the capacity to continuously improve their practices?**
- **How can the use of research knowledge be increased in schools and school districts?**

This list is intentionally short. The priorities it sets are consistent with, but significantly more focused than, the agenda for education research set by the U.S. Department of Education and its National Education Research Policy and Priorities Board. To be sure, the research literature covers many additional domains of knowledge; the reform movement embodies other worthy goals for American education, such as civic responsibility and arts experience. The committee chose these topics because they lie at the heart of education: together they hold potential for significantly improving student learning. They speak directly to the problems that teachers and school officials face every day. They address the most pressing concerns of parents and the general public. They have links to substantial bodies of underutilized research. They work together as a set—they could yield a mutually reinforcing set of answers. Not least, the four questions offer a conceptual framework that could weave together many existing research programs and reform efforts. The resources and energy invested in this strategic program of research could have a high payoff for American education.

• •

INCORPORATING RESEARCH ON COGNITION, LEARNING, AND DEVELOPMENT INTO EDUCATIONAL PRACTICE[1]

Until quite recently, understanding the mind—and the thinking and learning that the mind makes possible—has remained an elusive quest, in part because of a lack of powerful research tools. With theoretical and methodological developments over the last 3 decades, however, there has been an extraordinary outpouring of scientific work on the mind and brain, on the processes of thinking and learning, on the neural underpinnings of learning and cognition, and on the development of intellectual competencies. The new evidence has been drawn

---

[1]This section draws heavily on the discussion of the science of learning and its implications for educational practice in *How People Learn: Brain, Mind, Experience, and School* (National Research Council, 1999a) and *How People Learn: Bridging Research and Practice* (National Research Council, 1999b).

from diverse disciplines, including cognitive science, developmental psychology, linguistics, anthropology, neuroscience, philosophy, and information science.

Advances in the study of mind and brain, cognition, and development provide a rich context for thinking about education. What has been learned from all of these fields offers a new understanding of human learning and the characteristics of organized knowledge that can be used to promote effective comprehension and productive thinking. Cognitive science theories and experiments help in understanding the mind's functioning and the development of competence. The physical organ, the brain, is more visible than ever before, thanks to new neuroimaging and other technologies. Neuroscientists can actually see pictures of brain changes over time and brain variations during different activities and among different individuals. Developmental scientists have found imaginative ways to study the cognition of infants and small children; their work reveals infants as active, hungry learners with strong predispositions toward language and number and the ability to make distinctions between animate beings and inanimate objects.

One of the most important influences on contemporary learning theory comes from basic research on how experts learn and think in contrast to the ways novice learners approach new tasks and go about solving problems. For example, one of the characteristics of expert learners is that they consciously use mental devices to keep themselves on task and to obtain feedback about their learning, including the extent of their understanding, what else they need to know, if they need to repeat a step because they didn't quite "get it," and so on. These strategies of thinking about thinking—metacognition—can facilitate and enhance any learners' efforts to attain understanding (Simon, 1996).

This knowledge about the efficacy of metacognitive processes indicates how marked a departure current learning theory has made from the behaviorist models that prevailed for much of the twentieth century. The earlier theories focused on the relationships between observable stimuli and observable responses; little consideration was given to the processes of the learner's mind or the social and cultural context in which learning takes place. Yet the process of explicating higher order skills and the most effective means of cultivating such skills "... is precisely what we need to establish [as] a scientific foundation

> Advances in the
> study of mind and
> brain, cognition,
> and development
> provide a rich
> context for
> thinking about
> education

for the new agenda of extending thinking and reasoning abilities to all segments of the population" (Resnick, 1987a:7).

Today's learning scientists have shown that knowledge is the product of both an individual's cognitive activities and the supporting human culture (Stigler et al., 1989; Bruner, 1990, 1996; D'Andrade, 1995; Cole, 1996; Shore, 1996; Geertz, 1997; Strauss and Quinn, 1997). There is broad consensus that the context of cultural and social norms and expectations influence people's acquisition and uses of knowledge in powerful ways.

The portrait of human learning that is emerging from the new science of learning suggests approaches to pedagogy, instruction, curriculum, and assessment that differ significantly from those common in today's schools (National Research Council, 1999; Resnick and Klopfer, 1989). The path from learning research to effective classroom practice, however, is neither simple nor straightforward. It will require an intensive research effort, including school-based research.

There are many tantalizing avenues a Strategic Education Research Program might explore. The rest of this section discusses several of these avenues.

TEACHING THAT BUILDS ON STUDENTS' PRIOR LEARNING

Recent research in the fields of neuroscience, cognitive science, and developmental psychology has shown that the experiences children have in the early years are critical to later learning (Greenough et al., 1987; Dawson and Fischer, 1994; Shore, 1997). Young learners are far from the empty vessels to which they have often been compared. From the first weeks of life, young children begin to develop sophisticated concepts (whether accurate or not) to explain and organize the phenomena around them. Early experience creates strong convictions about how the world operates; faced with facts or notions that conflict with these convictions, young learners may react with disbelief that they are unwilling to suspend. Children will take impressive imaginative leaps to avoid relinquishing cherished misconceptions (see Vosniadou and Brewer, 1989). Faced with adults' explanations that the world is round, for example, some children hold onto their flat-Earth theory by envisioning a pancake on top of a ball. Formal instruction does not easily dislodge students' prior understandings; only by probing for and identi-

Young learners
are far from
the empty
vessels to
which they
have often
been
compared

fying students' prior knowledge, including misconceptions and misunderstandings, can teachers use instruction to move their students on to more accurate and more sophisticated levels of understanding (see the review by Mestre, 1994).

In other words, students come to school with preconceptions about how the world works. If that initial understanding is not engaged, students may fail to grasp the new information or concepts, or may learn for purposes of the test, but fail to transfer the learning to new situations (see National Research Council, 1999:Ch. 4).

The challenge for teachers is to build on children's early learning and promote the growth of conceptual knowledge. Teachers need to make time to hear their students' ideas and questions. They need to be on the lookout for the misconceptions that characterize children's immature thought and frame their learning. They need to be prepared to assess children's thinking abilities, to decide when to make connections between existing knowledge and school learning and when to help the child overcome misconceptions or naive understandings.

Teachers need to make time to hear their students' ideas and questions

TEACHING FOR DEEP UNDERSTANDING

Another line of investigation suggested by cognitive and learning research involves the development of pedagogical approaches that integrate the three critical elements of deep understanding: factual grounding, awareness of the structure of knowledge in a discipline, and metacognitive or self-monitoring activities.

Classroom teaching has often focused too narrowly on the memorization of information, giving short shrift to critical thinking, conceptual understanding, and in-depth knowledge of subject matter. As shown by numerous research studies, the development of intellectual competence requires more than the accumulation of discrete pieces of information. The elements of content that can be learned about a domain of knowledge are embedded in coherent structures. Indeed, the ability to discern and build on those structures distinguishes experts from novices in a given field. For example, experts in physics do not simply solve problems better or faster than beginning learners. They approach the problems differently, identifying similarities among problems based on major principles and laws of physics; in contrast, novices group problems according to the equations that can be used to solve them (Larkin, 1983). Helping students to recognize and build on knowledge structures is a crucial goal of teaching.

A student's capacity to function within a conceptual field will mature as he or she is helped to mesh different kinds of information, use them as a springboard for abstract thinking, and apply more rigorous forms of reasoning (Webb and Romberg, 1992). Curriculum can be thought of as a way to familiarize learners with the landscape of a knowledge domain or subject matter, so that they can negotiate the new terrain on their own and make effective use of its resources (Greeno, 1991). They need the kinds of learning activities that will help them talk, write, and think about the subject matter. By talking and listening to each others' thinking, learners gain the vocabulary, syntax, and rhetoric—the discourse—needed to understand and describe the knowledge structures associated with specific subjects and specific problems. They can gain greater capacity for metacognition—thinking about and gaining insight into their own thinking and learning processes. Helping students evaluate and regulate their own learning, using communication with peers and teachers as part of the process, can be effective in various domains (Carey, 1996; Treisman, 1996). Educational technologies can help students develop models of what they are learning. They make the learners' reasoning processes public and inspectable (Schauble, 1996; Chapman, 1996).

EFFECTIVE TRANSFER OF KNOWLEDGE TO NEW SITUATIONS

There is a wealth of research that helps illuminate the relationships between teaching approaches and students' ability to make use of what they have learned. Certain methods of teaching, particularly those that emphasize memorization as an end in itself, tend to produce knowledge that is seldom if ever used. Students who learn to solve problems by following formulas, for example, often are unable to use their skills in new situations (Redish, 1996). As a consequence, students often view school learning as irrelevant.

Students who have been afforded opportunities to generalize from their previous experiences (Klahr and Carver, 1988), who have learned with multiple examples, practiced their skills in a variety of situations, and discussed their ideas with others

Educational technologies can help students develop models of what they are learning

develop a much finer sense of what might be called the conditions of applicability of their knowledge. They know when to use it and when it is not appropriate, how to fine-tune it to make it appropriate to different circumstances, and how to develop strategies for addressing scenarios that differ from the primary case [Anderson et al., 1996; Ericcson, and Charness, 1994; Cognition and Technology Group at Vanderbilt (CTGV), 1997].

There are many implications for schooling in the research on transfer of learning. Much remains to be worked out in practice. A teacher's focus needs to be on helping students make connections between new and old knowledge. This means, in part, helping students approach learning situations in a deliberate fashion. A learner needs to see the relevance of the cognitive processes she or he controls, including processes of comparison, evaluating same/different distinctions, categorizing the new problem in terms of what seems familiar or unfamiliar, and so forth. The goal is to help students think about the specific challenges associated with new material, anticipate difficulties, evaluate feedback, and explain things to themselves to gauge their own progress toward understanding.

BUILDING AN ENVIRONMENT THAT SUPPORTS LEARNING

Learning has often been thought of as an individual—and perhaps solitary—activity. A number of powerful, new ideas for improving education derive from research on the interpersonal dimensions of learning, on cognition as a social process.

Several lines of research on the social context of learning have been inspired by the work of Vygotsky (1978). The emphasis shifts from the individual learner to the environmental supports for learning, including intellectual tools like language, other minds, and the surrounding culture with all of its symbols and rituals that help to organize events. These things—tools, people, culture—strongly influence what a person regards as meaningful (Egan, 1997).

Researchers who study how environments support learning and development argue that the human being at any point of development learns within the framework of meaningfulness. Researchers in the Vygotskian tradition believe that anchoring learning in specific situations taps a critical source of meaning, and they encourage connections between learning and one's

These things— tools, people, culture—strongly influence what a person regards as meaningful personal history. "Whether dealing in remembering, or the development of mathematical knowledge and problem solving within a cultural group . . . [we] need to ground theoretical statements and empirical claims in a unit of psychological analysis that corresponds to the lived events of everyday life" (Cole, 1996:220).

Cole's is one among a variety of new approaches in developmental science to call for more attention to settings (the ecology) in the study of learning and behavior (Bronfenbrenner and Morris, 1998). This represents a clear departure from older approaches to cognition that focused almost exclusively on the internal processes of an individual mind. The social perspective emphasizes the practical and social grounding of cognition in the structures of everyday activities and relationships (Suchman, 1987; Lave, 1988a, 1988b; Rogoff, 1990; Lave and Wenger, 1991; Wertsch 1991; Hutchins, 1995; Nardi, 1996). It focuses attention on a number of mechanisms of learning that did not emerge in earlier studies of individual cognition, on the internalization of social processes during learning. This research also has provided insight on how learning is guided and supported ("scaffolded") by more experienced individuals and how learners play an active role in their own development (Rogoff and Wertsch, 1984; Rogoff, 1986, 1990; Resnick, 1987b; Lave, 1988a, 1988b; Brown et al., 1989; Lave and Wenger, 1991).

The social perspective has had a significant effect on how classroom learning is studied, and it has produced research on local variations in classroom activities and organization (Heber, 1981; Heath, 1983; Rohlen, 1983; Cazden, 1988; Tobin et al., 1989). The social perspective has also focused scholarly attention on understudied populations of learners and revealed learning differences among children of differing social class and learning variations associated with race and ethnicity (Ginsburg, 1997; Brice-Heath, 1981, 1983).

A final variant on the theme of cognition as a social process is the idea of distributed cognition. When scientists hold laboratory meetings to discuss a project and share their ideas, experiences, successes, failures, and ideas for next steps, they share a knowledge of a subject that propels the discussion beyond procedural details to the substantive issues. Professionals and scientists frequently use a collegial mode of inquiry and interaction, having found that the exchange of ideas will lead to quicker and more effective solutions than individual work alone.

> Professionals and scientists frequently use a collegial mode of inquiry and interaction

Distributed cognition could prove to be an important construct for developing more successful ways of organizing classrooms and instruction. It is often cited as part of the promise of new computer-based educational technologies (Pea, 1993; Cognition and Technology Group at Vanderbilt, 1998). There is some evidence that this approach to learning can be an effective mechanism for classroom learning (National Research Council, 1999; Brown and Campione, 1994). In classrooms designed to encourage this approach to children's learning, researchers have discovered that even locating and defining a problem is often a joint enterprise (Wertsch et al., 1980). While some aspects of problem solving take place "in the head," many others take place "in the world."

Bits and pieces of the approach are visible in many schools in the use of aides and volunteers in the classroom, team teaching within and between schools, and the inclusion of community members and academic or industrial specialists in school activities. There have been some exciting experiments with programs like cooperative learning, but there is much to be learned about how to translate the insights from the research on distributed learning into programs that improve student learning in the average school.

INCREASING STUDENT MOTIVATION AND ENGAGEMENT IN LEARNING

Motivation research studies how individuals decide which tasks to engage in and what affects the persistence and intensity of their engagement. The problem is an intriguing one: Why do some individuals persist even when they are struggling, while others quit at the first sign of difficulty?

The issue is of fundamental importance. No amount of research and no attempts at reform are likely to strengthen learning unless students themselves are willing to work hard. The challenges of today's world require a level of knowledge and expertise that cannot be acquired without effort, even by the most able students. From the early grades, learners must exert themselves to pay attention, to carry out assignments, to study and review challenging material, and they must somehow be motivated to do these things.

Why do some individuals persist even when they are struggling, while others quit at the first sign of difficulty?

In general, more is known about how learning takes place than about the conditions and incentives that motivate students to expend effort and to achieve special goals. Although there is a lot of research on motivation, there is no commonly accepted unifying theory or even a set of agreed-upon principles and no systematic application of what is known to educational practice. This lack of knowledge is especially troubling in light of strong evidence that the great majority of American students are not paying as much attention to schoolwork or exerting as much effort as they could. A survey conducted by Public Agenda (1997), *Getting By: What American Teenagers Really Think About Their Schools,* indicated that two-thirds of teenagers readily admit that they could do much better in school if they tried. Half of the teenagers surveyed by Public Agenda say their schools fail to challenge them to do their best.

Other studies support these findings. For the *Mood of American Youth* (National Association of Secondary School Principals, 1996), American teenagers were surveyed about their attitudes toward various aspects of their daily life; the survey revealed far more positive attitudes toward friends, sports, and social activities than toward classes and learning. Does this matter? A study from the U.S. Department of Education's National Education Longitudinal Survey:88 investigated the relation between eighth graders' engagement with learning (including attendance, class participation, extra-curricular involvement, and several indicators of a students' identification with the school) and their school achievement. The survey shows a strong positive relationship between the degree to which school matters to students and the outcomes of schooling, and these relationships persist even when racial, socioeconomic, and home-language differences are controlled (U.S. Department of Education, 1990).

It is clear from this data, to say nothing of the everyday observations of teachers, that there is great variation in the motivation (willingness to expend effort) that students bring to their studies and, furthermore, that a very substantial proportion of children in schools expend only modest amounts of energy and time on learning. Achievement data indicate that a significant minority of children in schools expend only minimal effort on acquiring the skills and knowledge needed to participate fully in society as adults. If ways can be found to increase the amount of effort that students, and particularly young stu-

> Teenagers
>
> readily admit
>
> that they could
>
> do much better
>
> in school
>
> if they tried

dents, expend on learning, the effects on educational achievement would be exponential.

A large and potentially bewildering number of physical, psychological, social, and instructional variables have been examined for their possible influence on student engagement in learning; see Figure 1. Some of the themes that might be explored as part of a Strategic Education Research Program are discussed in the rest of this section.

EXPECTATIONS, EFFORT, AND PERFORMANCE

For school-age children, motivation to achieve is strongly related to their beliefs about the nature of intelligence and how it is acquired (Dweck and Elliot, 1983). If they believe in the malleability of intelligence and some internal locus of control (rather than fixed aptitude and luck or the actions of others), children will try and keep trying, even if they fail at first to master the academic content in a task; without that belief, many avoid trying altogether (Elliott and Dweck, 1988; see also Henderson and Dweck, 1990).

Cross-cultural research lends support to this view. An extensive study of elementary education in Japan, China, and the United States suggests that higher achievement in Asian countries results, at least in part, from a belief in the power of effort on the part of teachers, parents, and students (Stevenson and Stigler, 1992). This study emphasizes the role of parents, noting that U.S. parents are far less likely to subscribe to effort-based notions of achievement. The researchers note the propensity of U.S. parents to communicate low standards and accept less than optimal performance.

Children tend to solidify a sense of who they are academically and where they stand in relation to their peers when they are in the primary grades (Carnegie Task Force, 1996). The notions they form about their own capabilities, based on messages received from their family, school, community, and the popular media, can strongly influence their motivation to succeed and their later success. Societal messages about fixed aptitude associated with groups (by race, ethnicity, or gender) can be particularly oppressive. For example, African American students appear to resist intellectual but not athletic competition; constant messages about the academic inferiority of black students negatively affect black students' perceptions, resulting

Motivation to achieve is strongly related to . . . beliefs about the nature of intelligence and how it is acquired

	Physical	Psychological
Things that have a positive effect	• Good health/energy • Good nutrition • Adequate sleep • Adequate food and clothing	• Rational calculus that it's worth the effort • Self-confidence; belief one can succeed • Meaningful rewards • Awareness of process; sense of mastery • Encouragement • Attention from significant others (teachers, parents, etc.)
Things that have a negative effect	• Hunger • Fatigue • Being too cold or hot • Illness • Micronutritional deficiency • Poor general heath; low energy • Parasites • Drugs or alcohol	• Lack of attention from significant others • Perceived failure, ridicule, shame • Lack of rewards • Lack of confidence; expectation of failure • Rational calculus that it's not worth the effort

Learner

FIGURE 1 Variables that may affect student motivation. SOURCE: Adapted from materials

for many in avoidance of intellectually competitive environments (Howard and Hammond, 1985). A relationship between attributions of fixed aptitude to ethnic groups and students' performance has been demonstrated experimentally (Steele, 1992; Steele, 1997; Steele and Aronson, 1995).

If parental beliefs about the nature of intelligence and learning influence children's engagement in learning generally, parent's attitudes can also influence children's school performance in specific subjects or domains. The most studied domain is literacy (DeBaryshe, 1995; Spiegel, 1994). Researchers have shown that intrinsic motivation for reading is more likely to develop in homes where literacy is viewed as a source of entertainment and pleasure (Baker et al., 1995). This is an important finding, since studies of reading and motivation show that for school-age children, positive attitudes toward reading correlate with higher levels of reading achievement (Baker and Wigfield, in press).

Teachers' attitudes and expectations also influence students' motivation and achievement. In the late 1960s and 1970s there

Social	*Task Related; Educational*	
• Family socialization	• Cognitively appropriate	
• Social support system	• Appropriate level of difficulty	**Learner Activities**
• extended family	• Perceived relevance of task or	
• other adults	subject matter	
• role models	• Good pedagogy	Paying attention
• Family support and expectations	• active learning	Concentrating
• Peer group support	• Interesting task or subject	Trying to remember
• peer group competition	matter	Mentally rehearsing
		Thinking
		Practicing
• Lack of peer group support;	• Boring task or subject matter	Focusing on task
competition for attention	• Poor pedagogy	Persevering
• Distractions	• Purely passive learning	
• sports	• Work that is too easy or	
• TV	too difficult	
• social activities	• Lack of relevance	
• Competing demands, expectations		
• Negative role models		
• Lack of socialization in family		

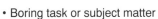

developed by committee member David A. Goslin.

were numerous studies of teacher expectations, including observational studies of classrooms, to determine how teachers interact with students that they perceive to be high or low achievers. One study (Brophy and Good, 1974) found that about one-third of classroom teachers show patterns of highly differentiated behavior: they call on low achievers less often to answer classroom questions or perform demonstrations, wait less time for them to answer questions, praise them less frequently after successful responses, criticize them more frequently for incorrect responses, and do not stay with them in failure situations (by providing clues or asking follow-up questions). Another study (Kerman, 1979) identified behaviors that teachers in Los Angeles were more likely to use with students whom they perceived to be high achievers; when they instructed those teachers to purposefully use those behaviors with low achievers, the result was improved performance.

Much remains to be discovered about the influence of adults' attitudes and expectations on children's motivation and engagement. More knowledge is also needed about how parents'

Teachers'

attitudes and

expectations

also influence

students'

motivation

and

achievement

and teachers' expectations arise; how their expectations relate to children's actual performance; how their behavior communicates expectations, evaluations, and rewards; and how that behavior affects children. Parents obviously influence their children's learning, but much more needs to be known about whether parent behaviors and attitudes can be changed, the kinds of interventions that can change them, and how much these interventions would ultimately improve student motivation and student learning (Baker et al., 1995).

There is also room for greater methodological rigor. Almost 20 years ago there was a warning that the educational literature "contains its share of loose thinking about expectations of lower-class and minority-group children, much of it based on fantasy rather than hard evidence" (Entwisle and Hayduk, 1982:164). The warning is as cogent today, as parents and policy makers look to standards-based reform to change the expectation levels for all students in order to motivate them to work harder and achieve more. The interaction effects are likely to be far more complicated than the public enthusiasm admits of. Without rigorous study and evaluation, standards-based reform is likely to become just another innovation that failed.

MOTIVATING BY DESIGN

A distinction is commonly made between motivation generated by the intrinsic interest or value of the material being studied and the creation of motivation through the use of extrinsic incentives, such as praise, grades, stars, or other rewards (Stipek, 1993). There is reason to think that both factors can be purposefully manipulated to increase student engagement. One line of research shows that intrinsic motivation can be enhanced through involvement in activities that are varied, engaging, social, and "authentic" (that is, related to real-world purposes or uses). For example, project-based learning, which allows small groups of students to work together on extended projects, can increase students' motivation to learn (Brown and Campione, 1996). Discovery learning, an approach developed by cognitive scientists to encourage students to discover for themselves concepts and connections which underlie a body of knowledge, can be more engaging than a traditional lecture (Simon, 1996).

But not every subject can be made intrinsically interesting to every student. If they are to expend sufficient effort on their schoolwork, most students sometimes need extrinsic incentives. Instructional designers have introduced specific strategies to increase student motivation. For example, cooperative learning methods have provided rewards to heterogeneous groups based on the performance of all of their members. This incentive system motivates students to encourage and support each other's learning (Slavin, 1995). If children are put in school environments that press them to invent, explain, justify, and seek out information, it will help socialize them to an effort-based notion of intelligence and thus promote achievement motivation (Resnick et al., 1996:19-20). Rewarding students on the basis of improvement over their own past performance has also been found to be an effective incentive system (Natriello, 1987; Slavin, 1980).

Analysis and experimentation are also focusing on the culture and structure of the school. A large-scale study of high-school students found that their motivation depends to a great extent on the quality of the relationships they experience. Students thrive when schools are organized in ways that assure continuity in their relationships with teachers and other adults (Lee and Smith, 1994). Ongoing work in District 2 in New York City, describes the measures designed to provide students with "an identification with the aims of schooling, a sense of belonging within a learning community, and a commitment—even a sense of responsibility—to participate actively in all learning activities" (Resnick et al., 1996:33). One design element is for instructional activities to focus on developing competence rather than just displaying current levels of ability.

These studies show something of the promise that the choice of pedagogical approach and the design of the instructional environment and materials can be positive factors in motivating students. They are a promising avenue for further research.

UNDERSTANDING STUDENT DISENGAGEMENT FROM LEARNING

A good deal of research attention has been given to documenting the disengagement of students when they are teenagers. Disengagement from school gains salience as students approach the levels of schooling where delinquency, dropout rates, and school-to-work transition become issues of immediate concern. Researchers who have focused on high schools

> Students thrive
> when schools are
> organized in
> ways that assure
> continuity in their
> relationships with
> teachers and
> other adults

(including Theodore Sizer, Arthur Powell, and David Cohen) have stressed the weakness of incentives for serious learning in the culture as a whole (Sizer, 1992). The role of tracking and retention in grade as levers of disengagement has also received a good deal of attention (Shepherd and Smith, 1989; Oakes, 1990, 1995). "A volatile mismatch exists between the organization and curriculum of middle grade schools and the intellectual, emotional, and interpersonal needs of young adolescents. [This situation] increases adolescents' levels of risk and their vulnerability to a wide array of socio-emotional problems and self-destructive behavior" (Felner et al., 1997:521).

There has been much less research on motivation in the first decade of life, despite substantial evidence that the problem of disengagement begins very early (Astone and McLanahan, 1991; Finn, 1989). Dropping out is not an isolated event that happens in high school; it is the culmination of a process of disengagement from school that can often be traced back to children's earliest encounters with school (Entwisle and Hayduck, 1982). In particular, the propensity to dropout has been linked to absenteeism in the primary grades, a history of poor academic performance in the early years, problems with social adjustment, and children's behavioral style, particularly aggressiveness (Ensminger and Slusarcick, 1992; Lloyd, 1978; Kaplan and Luck, 1977). There are strong ties between retention in grade in primary school and later dropping out, even with measures of academic performance controlled (Stroup and Robins, 1972; Lloyd, 1978; Cairns et al., 1989).

The transition into full-time schooling (entry into first grade) constitutes a critical period for children's academic development (Entwisle and Alexander, 1989, 1993). Research suggests that most children, including those considered to be "at risk" of academic problems, begin school with high hopes; yet by the time they reach grade four, many have lost their self-confidence. *Years of Promise*, a report by the Carnegie Task Force on Learning in the Primary Grades (1996:4), put it this way: "Something happens to many American children as they progress to and through the elementary grades—something elusive and disturbing: over the years, they lose their natural curiosity and their enthusiasm for learning." The effects of early disengagement can be devastating, especially in light of research showing that in the primary grades, children "are launched into achievement trajectories that they follow for the rest of their school

> Dropping out is
> not an isolated
> event that
> happens in
> high school

years" (Alexander and Entwisle, 1988:1). Some studies conclude that it is possible to identify future dropouts as early as the third grade (Lloyd, 1978).

MOTIVATION AND LEARNING

By and large, theoretically generated intervention programs and longitudinal studies of their effectiveness, especially the effect on achievement, are missing from the research on student motivation and engagement. It is an important area and it is complex. When, whether, how (or even if) to intervene with the child, the teacher, the parent, or the community to maximize effects on student learning are questions that are ripe for scientific study. A great deal more needs to be known about how to change student motivation and engagement for the better, but the work needs to be focused, with sustained efforts that emphasize the payoff for achievement. The theory and the tools for undertaking such projects have been steadily developing, and the time is ripe to find ways to use them.

It is becoming increasingly apparent that answers to the first question on our agenda (How can research on cognition, learning, and development be incorporated into education practices?) must articulate with issues related to this part of our agenda. Simon (1996) provides one instance of the intermingling of concerns:

> Discovery learning gets students to work on interesting situations that motivate them to discover for themselves certain underlying concepts and connections. Research on curiosity tells us that people will stop attending to a stimulus if it is so simple it becomes boring, or so complex it appears chaotic and meaningless. A well-designed discovery learning experience can introduce children to what scientists do and how they go about doing it and can be more motivating than a traditional lecture approach. But discovery learning is not an automatic motivator. Research indicates that in order to be effective, discovery learning experiences must strike the right balance between simplicity and complexity, build on the previous knowledge and experience of the learner, and offer opportunities for discovery at a pace that sustains student interest.

In sum, the existing knowledge base on motivation, though not inconsequential, is fragmented and has large gaps. It is clear that parents' and teachers' attitudes and expectations influence students' motivation and achievement, but there is much still to be learned about how their attitudes and expectations can be changed and the ways in which those expectations relate to children's actual performance. Motivation and engagement in the learning process are influenced by individual differences in students' development and interests, as well as by cognitive, affective, behavioral, sociocultural, and institutional factors; increased understanding is needed of the relative importance of, and relationships among the various influences. And little is known about the long-term effect on different students of instructional strategies designed to increase engagement and motivation, including those that make use of new technologies. Research suggests that motivation is related to the culture of a school and its students' identification with its aims and commitments, but more information is needed about the kinds of classrooms, schools, and school districts that achieve and sustain high motivation.

A strategic program of research in the field of motivation could synthesize the many strands of motivation research, seeding the process of integration and theory building, promoting and linking theory-based intervention programs designed to increase student engagement and motivation, along with longitudinal studies of their effectiveness.

TRANSFORMING SCHOOLS AND SCHOOL DISTRICTS FOR CONTINUOUS IMPROVEMENT

Education as an institution, like other organizations, is subject to enormous inertia, fixed in place by tradition and the political forces of school boards, community expectations, administrative capacity, unions, and finance systems. This research topic focuses on the issue of improving organizational functioning, that is, making schools and school districts more capable of learning from experience and from research, better able to develop consensual visions and plans, and more effective at adapting to changing conditions. If student learning is to be significantly improved, schools as organizations will have to be actively and constantly in the business of finding answers—

and even identifying the emerging questions before issues turn into entrenched problems.

Two strands of research address the problem of creating schools and school districts that have the capacity to enhance student learning, one on business organizations and one on schools and other educational institutions. In the for-profit sector, recent research on organizational effectiveness has centered on an organization's capacity to learn—that is, to acquire and distribute knowledge and to change in response to shifting conditions. From seminal work by March and Simon (1958), an expanding literature has documented the evolution, characteristics, and processes of a "learning organization" (Argyris and Schon, 1996; Kochan and Useem, 1992) and the type of "quality management" needed to create and sustain it (Deming, 1986). Among the useful ideas to emerge is that an organization predisposed to learn will develop processes for making tacit knowledge explicit so that knowledge—observations about manufacturing glitches or service problems, about work habits, about customers and suppliers—can be gathered, sifted, and applied.

The literature on learning organizations has focused attention on the idea of organizational culture. The work of industrial anthropologists, for example, has documented relationships between the way work is organized and the ability of organizations to be flexible and responsive to changing conditions. Researchers in organizational development have drawn on work in cognitive science, political science, psychology, sociology, and anthropology to study the relationship between group learning and individual learning and between culture and cognition (Simon, 1996; Brown and Duguid, 1996; Brown et al., 1989; Hutchins, 1995). In this sense, many of the ideas underlying studies of organizational learning are very much in accord with research on the nature of learning and motivation, discussed above.

None of this work is likely to produce a how-to manual for running a school or school district, but it does provide a useful framework for exploring the issues of aligning the institutional and bureaucratic aspects of education with teaching and learning goals. In addition, there are a large number of case studies from the learning organization movement that might provide fruitful analogies to illuminate the processes and problems of change in education organizations.

The second strand of research relevant to continuous improvement includes work in recent decades that has sought to identify the characteristics of effective schools (Murphy et al., 1985). Studies of school restructuring, including a number of large-scale, long-term studies, have provided insight on the effects of various reform strategies, the interactions among them, and the conditions under which they succeeded in improving student learning (Felner et al., 1997; Newmann and Associates, 1996).

There is a growing consensus that policy and structural changes alone will not significantly improve student learning; capacity building at the local school is essential (Consortium for Policy Research in Education, 1996; Elmore, 1996; Tyack and Cuban, 1995; McLaughlin, 1991a, 1991b). High levels of student achievement flourish when the *culture* of the school and its *organizational structure* are compatible and are mutually supportive of the hard work of students and teachers (Newmann and Associates, 1996; Elmore and Burney, 1997). A structural change in the length of classes from 45 minutes to 90 minutes, for example, will have little effect on increasing student achievement unless teachers know and use pedagogical techniques that engage students in active learning experiences (e.g., examination and discussion with peers of primary source materials, collaborative problem solving) and students are prepared for active learning.

> **Policy and structural changes alone will not significantly improve student learning**

While the literature associated with organizational development describes learning organizations, research on schools often speaks of learning communities. Drawing on theory and practice in developmental psychology and cognitive science, this research proposes that children learn best in the context of caring and collaborative relationships (Carnegie Task Force on Learning in the Primary Grades, 1996). In response to these ideas, some communities are creating smaller schools (or schools within schools), where students are well known by their teachers.

An associated theme is the development of a professional community among teachers and administrators, among school districts and schools, characterized by such things as shared values, collaboration, shared decision making, professional development, and taking collective responsibility for students' learning. One study of successful professional communities in five inner-city schools analyzed both the characteristics of their professional relationships that appear to contribute to their success and the supportive structural conditions—time to meet and talk, interdependent teaching roles, the power to make decisions (Louis et al., 1995a, 1995b).

Elmore and colleagues (Elmore and Burney, 1997) argue that a well-developed professional community is one of the most important elements in restructuring schools to increase their capacity to implement a demanding intellectual curriculum. Newmann and Wehlage (1995:30) identified three characteristics of professional communities associated with higher levels of student achievement: clarity of shared purpose; collaboration to implement the shared purpose; and collective responsibility for student learning (see also Ball, 1997; Putnam and Borko, 1997; Resnick et al., 1991). The sustained collaborative work of teachers, researchers, and administrators at the school and district level in reform experiments is beginning to provide empirical evidence that supports the notion of professional community.

There are numerous examples of the importance of a well-developed professional community to make structural changes effective. Instituting participatory decision making, for example, produces only superficial changes in a school's power relations (Malen et al., 1990; see also Weiss, 1995). But in schools that have a strong moral commitment to high intellectual standards for students, shared decision making supports the professional community, which in turn is related to student achievement (Newmann and Associates, 1996). School size is another example. Small secondary schools in particular can have a positive influence on student achievement gains (Lee and Smith, 1995; Lee et al., 1995). Size appears to promote respect and trust between teachers and students, but the effect is most likely to be achieved in schools where teachers assume collective responsibility for student learning and there is a highly developed professional community in the school (Newmann and Associates, 1996).

A professional community in a school is an obvious community, but teachers and administrators are also members of the professional communities within a school district. One Philadelphia district made an effort to develop a common culture among the professionals in elementary, middle, and high schools so that continuous support for student achievement could transcend the individual school building level (Newburg, 1991).

The idea that school districts should nurture culture and professional communities within itself is relatively new. Yet, as the literature on organizational culture and organizational change makes clear, coherence and alignment of goals and community norms are critically important for systemic reform initiatives.

Schools and school districts in many parts of the country are engaged in strenuous efforts to transform themselves. There is much that is interesting, and some experiments are exciting, as the ongoing study of District 2 in New York City (Resnick et al., 1996) illustrates. Yet there is a fragmented quality to all of this activity that the existing research base cannot knit together. Education research needs to find a new paradigm if it is to produce major advances in our understanding of how schools and school districts function and how they can be made more effective as organizations. This will require the collaboration of researchers in organizational sociology, social psychology, political science, and education. It is, despite recent calls for a new academic discipline called "change science" (Wilson and Barsky, 1998:246), a collaboration unlikely to occur on its own, but which is conceivable within the framework of the Strategic Education Research Program described in Chapter 3.

PROMOTING THE USE OF EDUCATION RESEARCH TO IMPROVE STUDENT LEARNING

At the core of the SERP proposal is the conviction that, above all else, knowledge is needed on how to get research attended to by educators. The gap between research and practice in the field of education has been well documented. Research conducted in the 1980s showed that most teachers use a narrow repertoire of instructional practices; they expand that repertoire only when they are given substantial and carefully designed training (Sirotnik, 1983; Goodlad, 1984). Teachers are less able or willing to use relevant research findings than are members of other professions; medicine and law, for example, traditionally rely on research and development to inform practice (Fleming, 1988). And, indeed, nothing in their background prepares teachers to be consumers of research, with the result that teachers tend to be wary of research, believing—not with-out reason—that for the most part it has little potential for improving practice, is too remote from the classroom, fails to reflect their needs, and is not user friendly. In one survey of teachers, less than half of them agreed that education research gave them practical suggestions for improving instruction (Fleming, 1988).

These findings are troubling, not least because much of the research on cognitive development, motivation, and organizational change argues for instructional practices and systemic reform models that differ dramatically from traditional schooling. But these ideas have reached a very small percentage of the children now enrolled in the nation's 87,000 elementary and secondary schools (Elmore, 1996).

Some studies on this topic are characterized as "research to practice" studies; some are known as studies of "knowledge utilization in policy," and others as "policy implementation in practice." The problem with each of these formulations is that the relationships between research and its use are neither linear nor punctuated. Instead, the relationships are diffuse and complex, characterized at least by "sustained interactivity" (e.g., Huberman, 1989) and often characterized by processes labeled "knowledge creep" and "decision accretion" (Weiss, 1980, 1987).

Furthermore, research does not provide answers to all the questions of practice (Weiss, 1998a). What counts as knowledge when it comes to improving education is not merely the work product of those who identify themselves as researchers or evaluators. Important kinds of knowledge also arise in the insights and experience of policy analysts and policy makers and among teachers and administrators in schools. The use of knowledge emerging from research, policy, or practice is heavily constrained by the interactions of the different professional communities within the local context (McLaughlin, 1991b; McDonnell and Elmore, 1991).

One of the most important and consistent consensual findings in the knowledge-use literature is that the stereotypical "knowledge use" situation that people expect when first thinking about knowledge contributions to policy or practice is inaccurate. It is seldom the case that a specific social problem is solved by a decision to use the results of a research study. Naive assumptions about using research to find "what works" across the board are bound to bring disappointment (Weiss, 1998b). Commenting on the links between research knowledge and policy, Weiss (1991:308) notes:

> It probably takes an extraordinary concatenation of circumstances for research to influence policy decisions directly: a well-defined decision situation, a set of policy actors who have responsibility and jurisdiction for making the decision, an issue whose resolution depends at least to some extent on information, identification of the requisite informational need, research that provides the information in terms that match the circumstances within which choices will be made, research findings that are clear-cut, unambiguous, firmly supported, and powerful, that reach decision makers at the time they are wrestling with the issues, that are comprehensible and understood, and that do not run counter to strong political interests.

Knowledge use is more likely to be a process of "enlightenment" that is gradual, indirect, and interactive

Knowledge use is more likely to be a process of "enlightenment" that is gradual, indirect, and interactive, characterized by incremental changes that aggregate over time to become significant structural and substantive changes (Kirst and Jung, 1991). If information passes the filters in a social institution and is incorporated into practices or policy, the original "knowledge" becomes part of a broad system, informing views of what is or is not important, contributing to an implicit framework for devising solutions, and adding to a propensity to implement or customize different practices within the institution (cf. McLaughlin, 1991b). Given these complexities about knowledge use in education (or other social systems), is there any reason to believe that research findings discovered in one context are generalizable to other contexts? There is a school of thought that challenges the whole idea on the grounds that all findings are conditional and contingent, valid only in the immediate context from which they arose. This committee is more sanguine about the prospects of social science. There is enough commonality across people, programs, and organizations to make a functioning social world. Generalization is a reasonable—and necessary—pursuit (Weiss, 1998b). In this pursuit, we believe there are two distinct lines of inquiry and one mode of operation that are strong candidates for a strategic education research and utilization plan; they are outlined in the rest of this section.

USE OF RESEARCH FOR POLICY

• What dissemination channels are most effective in reaching policy audiences of different types (e.g., legislators, bureaucrats, administrators, school boards)?

• What are the conditions under which policy makers seek research or are receptive to research findings? The research to date suggests that it is during crises that policy makers look to research for help, when the issues are new and people have not made commitments on way or another, or when issues have been fought to a stalemate.

• If researchers knew better how to communicate with policy makers, would they be more receptive to research? Are there intermediaries who could be effective in developing better communications with education policy makers—e.g., think tanks, advisory commissions, consultants, the mass media? Under what circumstances are advisory commissions effective?

USE OF RESEARCH FOR PRACTICE

• Teacher research: The prevailing assumption is that teachers find research too unconnected to the classroom; but some teachers have undertaken research in their own classrooms.

—What conditions are necessary for teachers to undertake valid research: Collaborations with researchers? More control over their own time? School or school system support?
—If teachers do their own research, do they trust it? Do they use it? Does it make a difference to their practice?

• Pre-service and in-service education and training:

—If research findings about how people learn and how learners can be motivated are incorporated into teacher preparation, how much do the findings influence teachers' practice?
—Can positive effects be achieved with the existing teacher corps through in-service training?
—Does such training make teachers more receptive to other research?

• Research-based curricula:

—Can sophisticated research-based learning strategies such as the development of metacognitive skills be integrated into curriculum materials in a way that produces positive outcomes for student learning?

—If teachers are provided with curricula that are based on solid research on learning and motivation, are there observable effects on teaching practices and on student outcomes?

—What sorts of research-based curriculum materials are most effective in supporting teachers' acquisition of new pedagogical ideas, new teaching methods?

A COLLABORATIVE APPROACH TO RESEARCH

Donald Stokes (1997) has made a compelling case for a conception of research, both basic and applied, that would more effectively devote the country's research strength to unmet societal needs—what he calls use-inspired research. If no one quite yet knows how to improve the contribution of scientific knowledge to education, there is a better sense than before of how to find out. Huberman (1989) demonstrates the need for cycles of "sustained interactivity" in education in order to communicate to researchers the needs and contexts of teachers and to transfer new information to the community of practice. Based on an evaluation of numerous Canadian projects that involved partnerships between education researchers and practitioners from a variety of institutions, Cousins and Simon (1995) argue for a deeper partnership that involves collaboration in more aspects and phases of research and its use.

It is this sort of partnership that the SERP plan envisions at the core of a long-term program of research on improving the use of research knowledge in schools and school districts. And it suggests the final group of research questions:

• Is research that is the product of the collaborative efforts of researchers, practitioners, and policy makers more salient to the needs of the user communities?

• Are the research results generated by such collaborative projects more likely to be used in practice? Are teachers more open to the results? Are the results more effectively used?

- Do such collaborations help with the communication problem? Does the research get more effectively packaged so that it will engage policy makers directly? Are the findings of such collaborations easier for teachers to comprehend and integrate into their current thinking?

• •

CODA

"EVERY CHILD CAN LEARN"

The conviction that every child can learn to high standards has become the watchword of many practitioners and a dominant theme of today's education reform efforts. While it may sound bland, the statement challenges the widely held perception that some children have the innate ability to reach high performance levels while others are destined to be low achievers. It is the principle that fuels the standards-based reform movement—one of the important arguments for change in American education today.

In seeking to convince all of those involved in education to raise their expectations of individual students and groups of children, however, the standards movement courts danger. Unless education reformers can demonstrate, within a reasonable time, that all students can achieve at high levels, standards-based reform could backfire, convincing even today's most ardent supporters that only some children can learn. The need is therefore more urgent than ever to ensure that millions of teachers, and millions more prospective teachers, have the preparation, tools, and support they need to provide all children with real opportunities for learning.

It is not enough to say that every child *can* learn. More needs to be known about *how* every child learns. In other words, improving achievement on a broad scale requires fundamental knowledge about *how* learning takes place; *why* students are willing (or not willing) to do the hard work required for high achievement; and *where* students learn, that is, the characteristics of schools and school districts that facilitate and motivate high performance.

> More needs to be known about *how* every child learns.

The Challenge of Schools and School Districts with Diverse and Disadvantaged Students

Students who live in high-poverty and culturally diverse areas experience conditions at home, at school, and in the community that correlate with low academic achievement (U.S. Department of Education, 1996). The conditions endemic in many urban areas—high concentrations of poverty, family instability, crime, unemployment—complicate the process of education enormously. While test scores do not tell the whole story, they paint a bleak picture of the experience of poor children. Once a school has more than 40 percent low-income students, there are few programs that have a significant effect on achievement levels. Going to some schools risks failure in something as crucial as learning to read (National Research Council, 1998). Unless there is major change in the effectiveness of such schools, the situation can only become more critical. Demographic trends indicate that the growth of the youth population over the next 30 years will be concentrated in these at-risk areas.

Is it possible to address the questions we have identified for the SERP in high-poverty and culturally diverse contexts, given the intensity of the problems facing children, parents, and schools? The committee feels strongly that this is the challenge that makes the large investment of talent, time, and resources that SERP would entail worthwhile. The program should be consciously designed to address the challenges faced by educators and students in such school systems. Successes will not only provide lessons that are appropriate for students in any school, but will be the most compelling argument for the use of research in education.

3 | Getting Answers: Designing A Strategic Research Program

Designing a strategic research program for education is a difficult task. Improving the contribution of knowledge to education practices requires more than is encompassed in research-to-practice formulas as traditionally conceived. The challenge is understanding *how* to make improvements, understanding *when* knowledge can contribute to education. Moreover, the knowledge needed when it comes to improving social systems like education is not only the product of those who identify themselves as researchers; important kinds of knowledge also come from the halls of policy and from school teachers and administrators. Yet the kind of collaborative creativity that is the key to solving most complex problems—including that of improving student learning—is as difficult to effect among these separate professional cultures as it is essential (Pressman and Wildavsky, 1973; McLaughlin, 1991b; McDonnell and Elmore, 1991).

This strategic plan envisions building a collaborative effort focused on a small set of very important problems to improve the contribution of scientific knowledge to education. It will require participants with diverse expertise and viewpoints to develop a workable common language and a shared agenda. A program of research that aims to be strategic cannot apply the model of individual, field-initiated research projects that has characterized education research in recent decades: it must be much more focused and coherent. At the same time, the directed, highly specified approach to research that has been so effective in military research and development (R&D) and certain other high-technology fields is not well suited to this task—the research effort must be more flexible, more able to learn incrementally.

An educational
intervention
. . . has to be
incorporated
into a
highly complex
social system

The National Institutes of Health (NIH) research program offers a more promising model: by drawing on the two research traditions, it combines central program direction designed to advance public health with robust field-initiated project development. In doing so, NIH has embraced an approach to research that has advanced fundamental understanding of biomedical processes (e.g., the mechanisms that transform healthy cells into malignant ones), while also being responsive to public calls for better medical treatments—the so-called war on cancer (Stokes, 1997:137-138). But there are important aspects of medical research that reduce the salience of the NIH model to education. Perhaps most striking is that there are no equivalents of pharmaceutical companies to support education research. And an educational intervention is not like a drug or a serum: in education, even when you have a promising intervention, it has to be incorporated into a highly complex social system.

A NEW MODEL FOR EDUCATION RESEARCH

Making research more useful for education requires a new approach, combining the best features of the two research traditions and crafted to suit the nature of the complex social organism called the education system. We believe that this new approach has six crucial features:

(1) promotion of collaborative and interdisciplinary work;
(2) provision of constant, ongoing commitment on the part of core teams of researchers;
(3) a built-in partnership with the practice and policy communities;
(4) iterative and interactive interplay between basic and applied research in a structure that combines the richness of field-initiated research and the purpose of program-driven research;
(5) a plan that is sustained over a long enough time for results to be cumulative; and
(6) an overall structure that is cumulative in nature—each step planned to build on previous steps.

Given the decentralized character of education and the diffuseness of the federal research effort, the problem is how to get sustained attention over a decade or more by the best researchers to a program that is attuned to the needs of the policy and practice communities. The committee considered a range of possible mechanisms, but ultimately found the MacArthur networks of greatest interest. Envisioned as an "experiment in scientific organization," the MacArthur Foundation's Program on Mental Health and Human Development has been in existence for nearly two decades and has created 13 interdisciplinary networks (supported with long-term funding) devoted to addressing key challenges in the fields of mental and physical development and health (Kahn, 1993; Bevan, 1989; Prager and Kahn, 1994).[1]

At the core of the MacArthur model is the insight that complex social problems can only be effectively addressed through interdisciplinary research. Yet both academic structures and incentive systems and federal funding mechanisms militate against sustained investigations that transcend disciplinary boundaries. The networks were devised as a way to promote effective collaboration across the biological, behavioral, and social sciences, to encourage scientists from many disciplines to make common cause to understand complex social processes and to translate that understanding into practical benefits (Kahn, 1993:iii).

Foundation funds are used primarily to facilitate communication and collaboration among the network members (technology, meetings, etc.), as well as some collaborative research projects. The foundation does not typically support projects being conducted by individual members of the teams, but it does fund some big network projects. In the case of the Successful Midlife Development Network, for example, the foundation provided funding for a major survey that has generated a wealth of data for all members of the network (and others) to exploit.

The 13 MacArthur networks evolved over the years as the foundation learned from experience. Some were more successful than others; some endured while others did not; some

---

[1]In addition to published sources, the committee benefited from personal communications from people involved with the MacArthur networks, including Orville Brim, Grace Costellazo, John Monahan, Dennis Prager, Ann Marie Palincsar, and Ruth E. Runeborg.

became the springboard for rich interdisciplinary collaborations while the influence of others was transitory. A great deal was learned about intellectual collaboration and about the elements of success. And there is evidence that the networks have produced an array of innovative methods, significant data sets, and important findings. Perhaps most important, network members describe the excitement and creativity unleashed by collaborations across areas of expertise, which challenge the old assumptions and mental ploys that often hamper innovative research.

The plan that follows is obviously deeply indebted to the MacArthur networks, but there are some differences worth noting. The MacArthur networks had a strong basic research orientation, although the foundation was also deeply concerned about applications. The SERP plan would reverse the emphasis. And in an important sense the SERP idea is more ambitious—and risky—for it expands the goal of collaboration beyond scientific disciplines to include the expertise of policy and practice. If successful interdisciplinary collaboration requires researchers to adapt to one another's professional culture, intellectual traditions, and analytical methods—and the MacArthur experience shows that this is not easy, then how much more challenging it will be to create successful collaborations of scientists, practitioners, and policy makers. It is, nevertheless, essential if the potential of education research to improve practice is to be realized.

A final point for consideration has to do with the balance of research support. The MacArthur program was a high-leverage design that assumed that network members would have other sources of support for their individual research. SERP would not be able to depend on all network members, for example, practitioners, having independent support for their time spent on SERP activities. Nevertheless, SERP is designed to leverage existing investments in research. It would aim, for example, to draw in the technology centers of the National Science Foundation (NSF) and the regional laboratories and R&D centers of the Office of Education Research and Improvement (OERI) of the U.S. Department of Education as partners in advancing the work of the SERP networks.

SERP is
designed to
leverage
existing
investments in
research

THE SERP NETWORKS

We see the SERP mission carried out by four networks of expert and committed education researchers, working in collaboration with practitioners and policy makers. Their mandate would be both to pursue research and to develop strategies for getting the best available knowledge used in everyday education practice, all with the goal of improving student learning. Each network will address one of the four hub questions:

• The **Learning and Instruction Network** addresses the question: How can advances in research on human cognition, development, and learning be incorporated into educational practice?

• The **Student Motivation Network** addresses the question: How can student engagement in the learning process and motivation to achieve in school be increased?

• The **Transforming Schools Network** addresses the question: How can schools and school districts be transformed into organizations that have the capacity to continuously improve their practices?

• The **Utilization Network** addresses the question: How can the use of research be increased in school and school districts?

The committee accorded a special status to the utilization network. While all of the networks will be committed to promoting and studying the use of research findings relevant to the hub questions, this network will try to develop general principles for theory and practical guidance on how to remove barriers and facilitate the use of research knowledge in education practice. It will work closely with one or more of the other three networks on particular projects, using them as cases for learning and experimentation. Also important is for all four networks to confront the questions and serious problems that arise in attempting to implement research's best ideas in schools serving poor or underachieving students. If SERP can figure out how to substantially improve student learning in schools with the most problems, it will be the key to getting every teacher, school, and school district interested in using research.

Core Components

Each network would have a director who devotes half time to the network. The director should be chosen on the basis of ability to address the network's hub question and skill at leading a team with members from diverse backgrounds. The commitment and leadership of the directors will probably be the single most important factor in making SERP work. The core membership in the networks would range from 7 to 15 people from different institutions and from different disciplines and professions. It is essential that the network members be creative, committed, and productive people, open to the possibilities of collaborative work and ready, as Kahn (1993:19) put it, to "make a sustained effort to link their work and their ideas to those of others."

At the outset of SERP, each network director would work with a governing board of the whole to develop a general 12-year plan. The keystone of each network plan would be a synthesis of the state of knowledge and the extent of knowledge utilization within its domain.

The MacArthur experience suggests that the members of each network would need to meet as a group at least four times a year. The network as a whole would work together to design and evaluate projects that advance the network objectives, solving problems and maximizing the chances for impact on the network's hub questions. Between network meetings, the members would communicate regularly by telephone and computer communications and work as needed in subgroups with task forces on specific projects.

Network Strategic Plans

Each network would be responsible for carrying out three key functions: (1) assessing the state of knowledge and the extent of knowledge utilization within its domain; (2) expanding that knowledge base by undertaking and commissioning research, with an emphasis on "usable" research; and (3) increasing knowledge utilization in districts and schools, in collaboration with the utilization network.

Each network would produce a strategic plan for achieving its mission and carrying out its key functions. An important starting point would be a critical synthesis of existing research, practice, and policy relevant to the network's hub question. A basic version would be developed during the start-up period for the network. A part of each network meeting and each network activity would be spent *revising* that synthesis through the incorporation of new developments from the network's activities, the interlocking networks of SERP, and the field at large.

An essential design element of SERP is that it is cumulative in nature—that new work takes advantage of and builds on earlier findings. The ongoing synthesis represents a concrete expression of that cumulation of understanding. The syntheses will identify and analyze:

- Strengths of the research base: What is known? With what level of confidence?
- Gaps in knowledge: Cases of problems that have been well documented (by practitioners, policy makers, or researchers) for which the existing knowledge base provides few workable solutions.
- Unused and underused knowledge: Cases where there is authoritative professional consensus on research findings or best practices, but applications have not yet been developed or are not as widespread as they should be.
- Incipient knowledge in the field: Cases where there is progress toward consensus on research findings or best practices, but further development and research are needed before applications can be confidently promoted.
- Productive conflicts in the field: Cases where the development of data, instruments, or theory would resolve conflicting claims and permit research and development to proceed.
- Barriers to and facilitators of utilization: The social, institutional, and individual factors that can work either as barriers or facilitators of the use of research findings. Each network will track specific cases concerning its hub question but will also plan joint work with the utilization network to identify and address potential barriers or facilitators.
- Priorities for the network: On the basis of the analysis described in the first five parts of the synthesis, agreement on the areas of greatest need and greatest opportunity for making progress on the hub question. Planned objectives for the network will be stated.

Each year's synthesis is a crucial step in the strategic planning process, but is not an end in itself. Based on this synthesis, each network plan would identify the areas of greatest need and greatest scientific opportunity and develop activities (both research and implementation) that have the greatest potential for making progress on the hub question. Planned objectives could be organized in a nested set with very specific yearly objectives for the first 4-year phase and more general ones for later phases.

NETWORK ACTIVITIES

Each network would undertake to meet the objectives identified in its strategic plan. Working within and across networks, the members would carry out a variety of activities.

Assessing the State of the Art Quarterly network meetings will serve as forums, where core members would present, discuss, and assess research, policies, and programs related to the network's hub question. These meetings would also serve as planning sessions for activities aimed at expanding knowledge or increasing its utilization on the hub question.

Furthering Research Each network will carry out research activities in its domain, consistent with the mission of SERP. This work might be done solely by network members or, more likely, by task forces headed by at least two members of a network with others from outside of network. The quality of the design and the results would be the responsibility of the sponsoring network. Undertakings might include, for example, reanalyzing existing data sets to shape a new hypothesis; replicating or expanding an effective but limited study; or conducting a study that tests a hypothesis under different conditions. Ideally, SERP would offer the opportunity and funding for centralized large-scale data collections. All network research would be expected to look beyond the traditional disciplinary boundaries and to take advantage of the full array of research fields, findings, and methods relevant to each hub question. Network research would also be expected to be informed by the needs and perspectives of the users and to meet accepted standards of excellence.

Strengthening Practice Task forces convened by networks could carry out activities aimed at enhancing instructional practice in K-12, consistent with the SERP mission. These might include, for example, running brief pilot studies to gauge the viability of a proposed multiyear project; coordinating with developers and practitioners to develop or evaluate promising materials; or sponsoring a design competition to produce several good solutions for well-defined problems in schools. All network activities and products will be expected to meet rigorous standards of excellence within the disciplines and professions.

Enhancing Existing Projects Some projects will be directed and funded by the network from start to finish. Other projects, however, could be carried out as a part of the ongoing activities of a core network member (funded by another private or public agency) or another research group or program. In such cases, the network might add components to planned or ongoing work, increasing the value of projects outside the network while fulfilling network objectives. For example, the network might support a set of questions piggy-backed on an existing survey; it might enhance a study by providing longitudinal evidence on a specific finding; or it might extend a study to test it under varying conditions. By enhancing existing projects, networks would cement relations with others in the field while making the most of their expertise and resources. This is one way in which SERP would operate on a wider scale or for a longer period than it could on its own.

Disseminating Network Findings and Activities The networks would be encouraged to use electronic and print media in an aggressive dissemination program. Publication of the annual synthesis from each network and, at the end of each 4-year period, the collected synthesis documents would be part of the dissemination effort. A SERP congress would be held periodically for network members to discuss their progress and findings with leading members of the research, practitioner, and policy communities. Congress proceedings and specialized materials could be prepared for targeted audiences, to translate network findings and recommendations into guidance for users. Network members would contribute articles based on network projects to professional journals and make presentations at conferences. Technology offers important opportunities, and the growing popularity of the Internet suggests the possibility of creating not just web pages devoted to network activities, but also databases for educators (theory-based curricular materials) and students (learning activities designed to promote deep understanding).

Building Capacity Within the Field Each network would undertake activities aimed at building capacity within the field to further education research and its increased utilization by districts and schools. For example, networks might establish task forces to develop human resources, data banks, or survey instruments intended to extend beyond the life span of SERP. These might include:

- workshops cosponsored by professional associations (e.g., American Federation of Teachers, the National Education Association, the International Reading Association, the National Association of Elementary School Principals, the Council of Chief State School Officers, the National Governor's Association);
- summer institutes cosponsored with universities and state departments of education;
- preprofessional courses offered through teacher education institutions;
- professional development sequences cosponsored with local school districts and state departments of education;
- mid-career fellowships to expand the capabilities of researchers, practitioners, and policy makers by immersion in the activities of the networks;
- data banks useful for researchers, practitioners, and policy makers who want to address questions about cognitive development, learning, motivation, etc.; and
- instruments to measure learning that would be sensitive to changes in student performance and causally related to changes in instructional situations.

RELATION TO OTHER PROGRAMS

The menu of network activities outlined above is very ambitious. It is important to reiterate that the intention is not to replace other education research and reform programs, but to strengthen the contribution of research to education by providing a powerful focus for related activities and by finding unrealized synergies. The SERP networks are not expected to be primarily a conduit for resources, but rather, a vehicle for focusing the attention and energies of the research community, sponsors, practitioners, and other stakeholders. For example, the annual syntheses—and the discussions they generate—could

These collaborations will unleash creativity and an excitement that could spread far beyond SERP

help weave together the programs of many different sponsoring agencies. The interdisciplinary character of the network activities promises to produce innovative approaches, new ways of looking at education and learning that can be incorporated by others and, if the MacArthur experience holds true, these collaborations will unleash creativity and an excitement that could spread far beyond SERP.

If it is not intended to replace other education research and reform programs, a successful SERP could nonetheless have a profound influence on research and practice. Its focus on four questions studied in national networks over 15 years would affect the organization of knowledge in education. This has implications for such things as graduate training, academic publishing, the allocation of new faculty positions. Furthermore, by building better bridges between the practitioner and research communities, SERP could illuminate the most productive avenues for investments in use-inspired research, and thus affect the research priorities of funding organizations.

• •

GOVERNANCE

We make no attempt in this document to say where the governance of the Strategic Education Research Program should reside, or even to say whether it should be public or private or some combination of the two; there are too many potential participants and possible locations for that to be sensible at this stage. But it is an issue of tremendous importance to the success of SERP. Could government provide leadership for a long-term, strategic research program? Would an agency like the Department of Education's Office of Educational Research and Improvement, which would seem a logical place to lodge such a program, have the political continuity or indeed the authority to enter into the kinds of agreements needed to sustain a 15-year effort? Would some sort of interagency partnership be feasible? Would a federal-state partnership offer advantages? Do the federal procurement regulations afford the flexibility needed to empower the thoughtful research managers so vital to the success of SERP? Would a consortium of foundations be a more likely alternative? Would leading foundations be willing to give up some of their autonomy to join forces in a strategic program. What are the serious bottlenecks likely to exist in the relevant public and private institutions, and can they be overcome? Could a public-private partnership be constructed that would enable the sponsoring institutions to make the most of the SERP idea.

All of these are questions for another day. Nevertheless, there must be a host organization, and we have given thought to the characteristics that it will need to embody.

HOST ORGANIZATION

In order to assure continuity, focus, coordination, mutual reinforcement, and quality control, SERP will need to be carried out under the auspices of a host organization. The host will need to be nationwide in scope, to have the capacity and experience to work over time with multidisciplinary groups, and to influence the dispersed world of education. Also, it will need to be prepared to make the connections between research, policy, and practice. The host organization will need to have the status, structure, and longevity needed to initiate SERP and to administer, monitor, and maintain it for a sustained period; it must also be able to provide the corporate structure needed for legal, fiscal, human resource, development, and public interface functions.

The nature of the host organization will have implications for the location of the networks and their relation to the host. It might be in a position to manage the networks in-house, or it could make sense to place their management in other institutions, for example, the director's university, or a research organization, or an entity like the OERI centers. The entire question of governance requires more thought and discussion by the interested parties, with particular attention to arrangements that will promote the coherence of the overall program and its ability to build cumulatively on the ongoing work.

SERP GOVERNING BOARD

To maintain the strategic nature of SERP, the host organization will need to establish a governing board to function as a policy board and also have coalition-building and development responsibilities. The governing board we envision would be capable of sophisticated and sustained interface with constitu-

> The entire question of governance requires more thought and discussion by the interested parties

encies, stakeholders, and decision makers in education. We believe the governing board would need to have at least 16 members, drawn in roughly equal proportion from four categories:

- policy makers—from local, state, and federal governments, and from nongovernment organizations (businesses, professional organizations) that support improvement in education;
- practitioners—teachers, school-level administrators, and district-level staff;
- researchers—whose work is relevant the hub questions; and
- fundraisers—leaders in foundation, business, government, and other spheres who would shape the campaign to generate financial support for SERP.

Policy Activities

The Governing Board would set overall policy for the Strategic Education Research Program. Among its policy activities, the board would:

- develop and refine the SERP mission and mandate;
- establish criteria for selecting and evaluating network personnel, select network directors;
- develop criteria for reviewing proposals and reports, upper and lower limits for the duration of networks, the number of network members and amount of honoraria for each, the percent of salaried time for the network directors and central staff, and the proportion of expenditures for administrative and substantive aspects of the program;
- assess the progress of the overall program at specified intervals, using independent reviews as needed, and correcting its course as needed; and
- promote strong linkages among the networks to assure the overall coherence of SERP.

The Board and the Networks The governing board would work with each of the networks in three ways: appointing the network director, reviewing each network's plans and allocating financial support, and assessing progress for each network. Annually, each network would provide the board with a substantive written and financial report and a plan for the following year's activity. Each network would also contribute to the board's 4-year reviews of SERP as a whole; these reports will be the building blocks for a quadrennial SERP congress.

In defining the relationship between the networks and the host organization, a careful balance needs to be struck between flexibility and coherence. The governing board and its staff would need to promote coherence and integration of the network activities so that together they advance the SERP mission.

SERP Congress The governing board would convene a national congress every 4 years, inviting the various stakeholders in education to participate. Each of the four SERP networks would present an updated report on the state of the art and conditions of knowledge use related to its hub question. Formal comment and discussion of these reports would be prepared by other network directors, board members, and key scholars outside of the networks. Following critical discussion at the congress, the board would prepare a response to the proceedings, charting new plans as needed for the subsequent periods of SERP's operation.

The quadrennial congresses would be a useful device for focusing attention on the most promising advances in research and development. The board might issue a series of reports addressed to diverse audiences for SERP—practitioners, policy makers, and researchers—ensuring, in particular, that policy makers and practitioners have the concrete detail and motivation to carry out changes that can improve student learning.

Development Activities

A central undertaking of the governing board would be to generate the financial support and political will to carry out the Strategic Education Research Program. Both the size and the nature of SERP make it desirable to build a coalition of funders, spread among the parties who have a stake in the fulfillment of its mission. The federal government has long supported education research and would be an important member of the coalition. There are also a number of foundations, old and new, that have a strong interest in education and numerous business organizations concerned about the quality of tomorrow's workforce.

The states have, by and large, not had a strong tradition of funding education research. A high priority of the SERP governing board should be to involve each of the 50 states and the District of Columbia so that state and local policy makers and practitioners would be customers *and* shareholders in the program. This would, over time, cement a circle of supply and demand with respect to getting good research used in education.

TIME FRAME

The success of a Strategic Education Research Program is predicated on the willingness of political leaders and the public to make a long-term commitment to it. The committee strongly recommends that, if the program is implemented, it be done with the expectation that SERP will continue for *at least* 15 years—2 preparatory years, 12 years of operation for four networks, and a final year devoted to completing projects and ensuring that the impetus continues for using the best knowledge in education practice. (See timeline on page 65.) Research initiatives in education have tended to be so abbreviated that the planned time frame may seem long, but it is important to keep in mind that it is less than the time that it takes for one cohort of children to graduate from high school.

During the 12 years that the networks would operate, reviews would take place at 4-year intervals. The host organization and the SERP board would take advantage of the periodic reviews to make informed decisions about continuing or correcting the course of each network. These reviews would ensure accountability and allow plans for the next period to be refined.

• •

NEXT STEPS

In the preface to this report, National Academy of Sciences' President Bruce Alberts conveys his enthusiasm about the potential of the SERP idea and his hope that it will catalyze major new investments in educational research—both by federal and state governments and by foundations. As a first step in that direction, the National Academies propose to launch a year-long national dialogue during which the idea for a Strategic Education Research Program is discussed with all the professional groups concerned with education. The feasibility of the plan needs to be widely discussed. The general design features suggested in this report need to be forged into workable specifications for a large-scale, long-term research and development program. Above all, a year of dialogue is needed to see if this plan can generate the kind of political will and financial commitment that will be needed for its operation.

We call upon the federal government, and in particular the Department of Education and the National Science Foundation, major foundations whose mission includes improving education, state and local education leaders, and education research organizations to join in this year of dialogue to see if, together, we can transform the SERP idea into a productive collaboration to use the power of science to improve education in the United States.

PROPOSED 15-YEAR TIMELINE FOR SERP

Years 1-2   **Host Organization Establishes SERP Governing Board**
- Board organizes a planning process to refine the hub questions and identify network participants. Board staff to commission papers, hold workshops to "audition" potential chairs, identify potential network members, develop the initial documents that will seed the work of the four networks
- Board develops funding sources
- Board appoints chair of each network, works with chairs to identify network membership
- SERP website is created
- Four network framing documents are published

Years 3-6   **Networks Begin to Function**
- Networks prepare first annual synthesis document (year 3)
- Networks develop strategic plans (year 3)
- Networks hold four network meetings per year
- Networks undertake R&D activities
- Networks develop links with other networks and with other ongoing activities (OERI labs and centers, NSF technology centers, etc.)

Year 6   **Board Holds First SERP Congress**
- Board arranges public discussion and critique of network activities, findings, and involvement of user communities
- Board publishes congress proceedings and targeted reports
- Board evaluates the progress of each network and the interaction among the networks, decides if each should continue, and be reoriented

Years 7-10   **Networks Continue Building Their R&D Programs, Capacity-Building Activities, Links to Other Research and Reform Programs**
- Networks continue publication of annual synthesis documents
- Networks refine and elaborate strategic plan

Year 10   **Board Holds Second SERP Congress, Publishes Proceedings and Targeted Reports**
- Board makes decisions about continuation, redirection of networks

Years 11-14   **Networks Continue Their R&D, Leveraging, and Capacity-Building Activities**

Year 14   **Board Holds Third SERP Congress**

Year 15   **SERP Winds Down and Hands Off to Successor Organizations or Activities**

References

Anderson, J.R., L.M. Reder, and H.A. Simon
   1996   Situated learning and education. *Educational Researcher* 25:4(May)5-11.
Alexander, K.L., and D.R. Entwisle
   1988   *Achievement in the First 2 Years of School: Patterns and Processes*. Monographs of the Society for Research in Child Development 53(2).
Argyris, C., and D.A. Schon
   1996   *Organizational Learning*. Reading, MA: Addison-Wesley Pub. Co.
Astone, N.M., and S. McLanahan
   1991   Family structure, parental practices and high school completion. *American Sociology Review* 56:309-20.
Baker, L., R. Serpell, and S. Sonnenschein
   1995   Opportunities for literacy learning in the homes of urban preschoolers. Pp. 236-252 in *Family Literacy: Connections in Schools and Communities*, L.M. Morrow, ed. Newark, DE: International Reading Association.
Baker, L., and A. Wigfield
   in   Dimensions of children's motivation for reading and their relations
   press   to reading activity and reading achievement. *Reading Research Quarterly*.
Ball, D.L.
   1997   Developing mathematics reform: What don't we know about teacher learning—but would make good working hypotheses? Pp. 77-111 in *Reflecting on Our Work: NSF Teacher Enhancement in K-6 Mathematics*, S. Friel and G. Bright, eds. Lanham, MD: University Press of America.
Bevan, W.
   1989   *Beyond the Territorial Solution: On Collaborative Methodology in Scientific Research*. Chicago, IL: The John D. and Catherine T. MacArthur Foundation.
Brice-Heath, S.
   1981   Toward an ethnohistory of writing in American education. Pp. 25-45 in *Writing: The Nature, Development and Teaching of Written Communication* (Vol. 1), M.F. Whiteman, ed. Hillsdale, NJ: Erlbaum.
   1983   *Ways with Words: Language, Life and Work in Communities and Classrooms*. Cambridge, UK: Cambridge University Press.
Bronfenbrenner, U., and P.A. Morris
   1998   The Ecology of developmental processes. Pp. 993-1028 in *Handbook of Child Psychology, Fifth Ed. Volume 1: Theoretical Models of Human Development*, W. Damon, and R. M. Learner, eds. New York: Wiley.

Brophy, J.E., and T.L. Good
  1974 *Teacher-Student Relationships: Causes and Consequences.* New York: Holt, Rinehart and Winston, Inc.
Brown, A.L., and J.C. Campione
  1994 Guided discovery in a community of learners. Pp. 229-270 in *Classroom Lessons: Integrating Cognitive Theory and Classroom Practice*, K. McGilly, ed. Cambridge, MA: MIT Press.
  1996 Psychological theory and the design of innovative learning environments: On procedures, principles, and systems. Pp. 289-325 in *Innovations in Learning: New Environments for Education*, L. Schauble and R. Glaser, eds. Mahwah, NJ: Lawrence Erlbaum Associates.
Brown, J.S., and P. Duguid
  1996 Universities in a digital age. *Change* 28(4):10-19.
Brown, J.S., A. Collins, and P. Duguid
  1989 Situated cognition and the culture of learning. *Educational Researcher* 18:32-42.
Bruner, J.
  1990 *Acts of Meaning.* Cambridge, MA: Harvard University Press
  1996 *The Culture of Education.* Cambridge, MA: Harvard University Press.
Cairns, R.B., B. Cairns, and H. J. Neckerman
  1989 Early school dropout: Configurations and determinants. *Child Development* 60(6):1437-1452.
Carey, S.
  1996 Science Education as Conceptual Change. Paper prepared for the Committee on Developments in the Science of Learning for the Sciences of Science Learning: An Interdisciplinary Discussion. Department of Psychology, New York University.
Carnegie Task Force on Learning in the Primary Grades
  1996 *Years of Promise: A Comprehensive Learning Strategy for America's Children.* New York: Carnegie Corporation of New York.
Cazden, C.B.
  1998 *Classroom Discourse.* Portsmouth, NH: Heinemann.
Chapman, O.
  1996 Learning science involves language, experience, and modeling. Paper prepared for the Committee on Developments in the Science of Learning for the Sciences of Science Learning: An Interdisciplinary Discussion. Department of Chemistry, University of California at Los Angeles.
Cognition and Technology Group at Vanderbilt
  1997 *The Jasper Project: Lessons in Curriculum, Instruction, Assessment, and Professional Development.* Mahwah, NJ: Erlbaum.
  1998 Designing environments to reveal, support, and expand our children's potentials. Pp. 313-350 in *Perspectives on Fundamental Processes in Intellectual Functioning.* Vol. 1. S.A. Soraci and W. McIlvane, eds. Greenwich, CT: Ablex.
Cole, M.
  1996 *Cultural Psychology: A Once and Future Discipline.* Cambridge, MA: Harvard University Press.
Consortium for Policy Research in Education
  1996 *Public Policy and School Reform: A Research Summary.* CPRE Research Report Series, Report #36. Philadelphia, PA: University of Pennsylvania and Consortium for Policy Research in Education.

Cousins, J.B., and M. Simon
  1995   The nature and impact of policy-induced partnerships between re-
         search and practice communities. *Educational Evaluation and Policy
         Analysis* 18(3):199-218.
Cross, C.T.
  1989   *Report on the Laboratory Review Panel on the Pending Laboratory
         Recompetition.* Silver Spring, MD: Macro Systems, Inc.
D'Andrade, R.G.
  1995   *The Development of Cognitive Anthropology.* Cambridge and New York:
         Cambridge University Press.
Dawson, G., and K.W. Fischer
  1994   *Human Behavior and the Developing Brain.* New York: Guilford Press.
DeBaryshe, B.D.
  1995   Maternal belief systems: Linchpin in the home reading process.
         Journal of Applied Developmental Psychology 16(1):1-20.
Deming, W.E.
  1986   *Out of the Crisis.* Cambridge, MA: MIT Center for Advanced Engi-
         neering Study.
Dweck, C.S., and E.S. Elliott
  1983   Achievement motivation. Pp. 643-691 in *Handbook of Child Psychol-
         ogy, Vol. 4. Socialization, Personality and Social Development,* E.M.
         Hetherington, ed. New York: John Wiley.
Education Week
  1998   The urban challenge. *Education Week* 17(17):6.
Egan, K.
  1997   *The Educated Mind: How Cognitive Tools Shape Our Understanding.*
         Chicago, IL: University of Chicago Press.
Elliott, E.S., and C.S. Dweck
  1988   Goals: An approach to motivation and achievement. *Journal of Per-
         sonality and Social Psychology* 54:5-12.
Elmore, R.F.
  1996   Getting to scale with successful education practices. Pp. 294-329 in
         Rewards and Reform: Creating Educational Incentives That Work, S.H.
         Fuhrman and J.A. O'Day, eds. San Francisco, CA: Jossey-Bass Pub-
         lishers.
Elmore, R.F., and D. Burney
  1997   *Investing in Teacher Learning: Staff Development and Instructional Im-
         provement in Community School District #2, New York City.* CPRE/
         NCTAF Joint Report. New York: National Commission on Teaching
         and America's Future and Consortium for Policy Research in Educa-
         tion.
Ensminger, M.E., and A.L. Slusarcick
  1992   Paths to high school graduation or dropout: A longitudinal study of
         a first-grade cohort. *Sociology of Education* 65(2):95-113.
Entwisle, D.R., and K.L. Alexander
  1989   Early schooling as a "critical period" phenomenon. Pp. 27-55 in
         Sociology of Education and Socialization. Vol. 8. K. Namboodiri and
         R.G. Corwin, eds. Greenwich, CT: JAI.
  1993   Entry into school: The beginning school transition and educational
         stratification in the United States. *Annual Review of Sociology* 19:404-
         406.

Entwisle, D.R., and L.A. Hayduk
  1982 *Early Schooling: Cognitive and Affective Outcomes.* Baltimore, MD: Johns Hopkins University Press.
Ericsson, K.A., and N. Charness
  1994 Expert performance: Its structure and acquistion. *American Psychologist* 49:725-745.
Felner, R.D., D. Kasak, P. Mulhall, and N. Flowers
  1997 The project on high performance learning communities: Applying the land-grant model to school reform. *Phi Delta Kappan* March:520-527.
Finn, J.D.
  1989 Withdrawing from school. *Review of Educational Research* 59(2)117-142.
Fleming, D.S.
  1988 *The Literature on Teacher Utilization of Research: Implications for the School Reform Movement.* Andover, MA: The Regional Laboratory for Educational Improvement of the Northeast and Islands.
Geertz, C.
  1997 Learning with Bruner. *The New York Review of Books* April 10.
Ginsburg, H.P.
  1997 *Entering the Child's Mind: The Clinical Interview in Psychological Research and Practice.* New York: Cambridge University Press.
Goodlad, J.I.
  1984 *A Place Called School.* New York: McGraw-Hill.
Greeno, J.
  1991 Number sense as situated knowing in a conceptual domain. *Journal for Research in Mathematics Education* 22(3):170-218.
Greenough, W.T., J.E. Black, and C. Wallace
  1987 Experience and brain development. *Child Development* 58:539-559.
Heath, S.
  1983 *Ways with Words: Language, Life, and Work in Communities and Classrooms.* Cambridge, England: Cambridge University Press.
Heber, M.
  1981 Instruction versus conversation as opportunities for learning. In *Communications in Development,* W.P. Robinson, ed. London: Academic Press.
Henderson, V.L., and C.S. Dweck
  1990 Motivation and achievement. Pp. 308-329 in *Adolescence: At the Threshold,* S. Feldman and G. Felder, eds. Cambridge, MA: Harvard University Press.
Howard, J., and R. Hammond
  1985 Rumors of inferiority. *New Republic* September 9:18-23.
Huberman, M.
  1989 Predicting conceptual effects in research utilization: Looking with both eyes. *Knowledge in Society* 2(3):6-24.
Hutchins, E.
  1995 *Cognition in the Wild.* Cambridge, MA: MIT Press.
Kahn, R.L.
  1993 *An Experiment in Scientific Organization.* Chicago, IL: The John D. and Catherine T. MacArthur Foundation.
Kaplan, J.L., and E.C. Luck
  1977 The dropout phenomenon as a social problem. *Educational Forum* 42(1):41-56.

Kerman, S.
  1979 Teacher expectations and student achievement. *Phi Delta Kappan* 60(10):716-718.
Kirst, M., and R. Jung
  1991 The utility of a longitudinal approach in assessing implementaion: A thirteen-year view of Title I, ESEA. Pp. 39-64 in *Education Policy Implementation*, A.R. Odden, ed. SUNY Series in Educational Leadership. Albany, NY: State University of New York Press.
Klahr, D., and S.M. Carver
  1988 Cognitive objectives in a LOGO debugging curriculum: Instruction, learning, and transfer. *Cognitive Psychology* 20:362-404.
Kochan, T.A., and M. Useem, eds.
  1992 *Transforming Organizations*. New York: Oxford University Press.
Larkin, J.H.
  1983 The role of problem representation in physics. Pp. 75-98 in *Mental Models*, D. Gentner and A.L. Stevens, eds. Hillsdale, NJ: Erlbaum.
Lave, J.
  1988a *The Culture of Acquisition and the Practice of Understanding*. Report No. IRL 880-0007. Palo Alto, CA: Institute of Research on Learning.
  1988b *Cognition in Practice*. Cambridge, England: Cambridge University Press.
Lave, J., and E. Wenger
  1991 *Situated Learning*. Cambridge, England: Cambridge University Press.
Lee, V.E., and J.B. Smith
  1994 High school restructuring and student achievement: A new study finds strong links. *Issues in Restructuring Schools*, No. 7. Madison, WI: Center on Organization and Restructuring of Schools, Wisconsin Center for Educational Research, University of Wisconsin.
  1995 Effects of high school restructuring and size on gains in the achievement and engagement for early secondary students. *Sociology of Education* 68(4):241-270.
Lee, V.E., J.B. Smith, and R.G. Croninger
  1995 Another look at high school restructuring. In *Issues in Rrestructuring Schools*, No. 9. Madison, WI: Center on Organization and Restructuring of Schools, Wisconsin Center for Educational Research, University of Wisconsin.
Lloyd, D.N.
  1978 Prediction of school failure from third-grade data. *Educational and Psychological Measurement* 38:1193-1200.
Louis, K.S., S.D. Kruse, and A.S. Bryk
  1995a Professionalism and community: What is it and why is it important in urban schools? In *Professionalism and Community: Persepctives on Reforming Urban Schools*. K.S. Louis, D. Kruse, and Associates, eds. Thousand Oaks, CA: Corwin Press, Inc.
  1995b An emerging framework for analyzing school-based professional community. In *Professionalism and Community: Persepctives on Reforming Urban Schools*. K.S. Louis, D. Kruse, and Associates, eds. Thousand Oaks, CA: Corwin Press, Inc.
Malen, B., R. Ogawa, and J. Kranz
  1990 What do we know about school based management? In *Choice and Control in American Education*, Vol. 2, W.H. Clune and J. F. White, eds. New York: Falmer.

March, J.G., and H.A. Simon

    1958   *Organizations.* New York: Wiley.

McDonnell, L.M., and R.F. Elmore

    1991   Getting the job done: Alternative policy instruments. Pp. 157-185 in *Education Policy Implementation,* A.R. Odden, ed. SUNY Series in Educational Leadership. Albany, NY: State University of New York Press.

McLaughlin, M.W.

    1991a Learning from experience: Lessons from policy implementation. Pp. 185-195 in *Education Policy Implementation,* A.R. Odden, ed. Albany, NY: State University of New York Press.

    1991b The Rand agent study: Ten years later. Pp. 143-155 in *Education Policy Implementation,* A.R. Odden, ed. Albany, NY: State University of New York Press.

Mervis, J.

    1998   Mixed grades for NSF's Bold Reform of Statewide Education. *Science* 282(Dec. 4):1800-1805.

Mestre, J.P.

    1994   Cognitive aspects of learning and teaching science. Pp. 3-1 to 3-53 in *Teacher Enhancement for Elementary and Secondary Science and Mathematics: Status, Issues, and Problems,* S.J. Fitzsimmons and L.C. Kerpelman, eds. NSF 94-80. Arlington, VA: National Science Foundation.

Murphy, J., P. Hallinger, and R. Mesa

    1985   School effectiveness: Checking progress and assumptions, and developing a role for state and federal government. *Teachers College Record* 86 (4 Summer 1995):615-641.

National Association of Secondary School Principals

    1996   *The Mood of American Youth.* Reston, VA: National Association of Secondary School Principals.

National Research Council

    1992   *Research and Education Reform: Roles for the Office of Educational Research and Improvement,* R.C. Atkinson and G.B. Jackson, eds. Committee on the Federal Role in Education Research, Commission on Behavioral and Social Sciences and Education, National Research Council. Washington, DC: National Academy Press.

    1998   Preventing Reading Difficulties in Young Children, C.E. Snow, M.S. Burns, and P. Griffin, eds. Committee on the Prevention of Reading Difficulties in Young Children, Commission on Behavioral and Social Sciences and Education, National Research Council.

    1999a *How People Learn: Brain, Mind, Experience, and School,* J. Bransford, A. Brown, and R. Cocking, eds. Committee on Developments in the Science of Learning, Commission on Behavioral and Social Sciences and Education, National Research Council. Washington, DC: National Academy Press.

    1999b *How People Learn: Bridging Research and Practice,* S. Donovan, J. Bransford, and J. Pellegrino, eds. Committee on Learning Research and Educational Practice, Commission on Behavioral and Social Sciences and Education, National Research Council. Washington, D.C.: National Academy Press.

Nardi, B., ed.

    1996   *Context and Consciousness: Activity Theory and Human-Computer Interactions.* Cambridge, MA: MIT Press.

Natriello, G.
    1987   The impact of evaluation processes on students. *Educational Psychologist* 22:155-175.

Newburg, N.
    1991   Bridging the gap: An organizational inquiry into an urban school district. In *The Reflective Turn: Case Studies in and on Educational Practice*, D.A. Schoen, ed. New York: Teachers College Press.

Newmann, F.M., and Associates
    1996   *Authentic Achievement: Restructuring Schools for Intellectual Quality.* San Francisco, CA: Jossey-Bass Publishers.

Newmann, F. M., and G. Wehlage
    1995   *Successful School Restructuring: A Report to the Public and Educators by the Center on Organization and Restructuring of Schools.* Madison, WI : The Center on Organization and Restructuring of Schools.

Oakes, J.
    1990   *Multiplying Inequalities: The Effects of Race, Social Class and Tracking Opportunities to Learn Mathematics and Science.* Santa Monica, CA: The RAND Corporation.
    1995   Tracking, Diversity, and Educational Equity: What's New in the Research? Report prepared for the Common Destiny Alliance Consensus Panel Meeting, August. RAND, Santa Monica, CA.

O'Day, J.A., and M. S. Smith
    1993   Systemic reform and educational opportunity. Pp. 250-312 in *Designing Coherent Education Policy: Improving the System*, Susan H. Fuhrman, ed. San Francisco, CA: Jossey-Bass Publishers.

Pea, R.D.
    1993   Distributed multimedia learning environments: The Collaborative Visualization Project. *Communications of the ACM* 36(5):60-63.

Prager, D., and R.L. Kahn
    1994   Interdisiplinary colloaborations are a scientific and social imperative. *The Scientist* (July 11):12.

President's Committee of Advisors on Science and Technology
    1997   *The Use of Technology to Strengthen K-12 Education in the United States.* Washington, DC: President's Committee of Advisors on Science and Technology.

Pressman J., and A. Wildavsky
    1973   *Implementation.* Berkeley, CA: University of California Press.

Public Agenda
    1997   *Getting By: What American Teenagers Really Think About Their Schools.* New York: Public Agenda.

Putnam, R.T., and H. Borko
    1997   Teacher learning: Implications of new views of cognition. Pp. 1223-1296 in *The International Handbook of Teachers and Teaching*, Vol. 2, B.J. Biddle , TL. Good, and I.F. goodson, eds. Dordrecht, The Netherlands: Kluwer.

Redish, E.F.
    1996   Discipline-Specific Science Education and Educational Research: The Case of Physics. Paper prepared for the Committee on Developments in the Science of Learning for the Sciences of Science Learning: An Interdisciplinary Discussion. Department of Physics and Astronomy, University of Maryland.

Resnick, L.
    1987a *Education and Learning to Think.* Commission on Behavioral and

Social Sciences and Education, National Research Council. Washington, DC: National Academy Press.

1987b Learning in school and out. *Educational Research* 16:13-20.

Resnick, L.B., and L.E. Kloper

1989 Toward the thinking curriculum: Current cognitive research. *Yearbook of the Association for Supervision and Curriculum Development*. Alexandria, VA: Association for Supervision and Curriculum Development.

Resnick, L.B., J.M. Levine, and S.D. Teasley, eds.

1991 *Perspectives on Socially Shared Cognition.* Washington, DC: American Psychological Association.

Resnick, L.B., A.J. Alvarado, and R.F. Elmore

1996 Developing and Implementing High-Performance Learning Communities. Proposal for research prepared by the Learning Research and Development Center, University of Pittsburgh (Solitiation No. RC-96-1370).

Rohlen, T.

1983 *Japan's High Schools.* Berkeley, CA: University of California Press.

Rogoff, B.

1986 Adult assistance in children's learning. Pp. 27-40 in *The Contexts of School-Based Literacy*, T.E. Raphael, ed. New York: Random House.

1990 *Apprenticeship in Thinking: Cognitive Development in Social Context.* New York: Oxford University Press.

Rogoff, B., and J.V. Wertsch, eds.

1984 *Children's Learning in the "Zone of Proximal Development."* San Francisco: Jossey Bass.

Schauble, L.

1996 The Development of Model-Based Reasoning in Elementary School Students. Paper prepared for the Committee on Developments in the Science of Learning for the Sciences of Science Learning: An Interdisciplinary Discussion. Wisconsin Center for Education Research, University of Wisconsin, Madison.

Shepherd, L.A., and M.L. Smith, eds.

1989 *Flunking Grades: Research and Policies on Retention.* New York: Felner.

Shore, B.

1996 *Culture in Mind: Cognition, Culture, and the Problem of Meaning.* Oxford and New York: Oxford University Press.

Shore, R.

1997 *Rethinking the Brain: New Insights into Early Development.* New York: Families and Work Institute.

Simon, H.A.

1996 Observations on the Sciences of Science Learning. Remarks delivered at meeting of the Committee on Developments in the Science of Learning for the Sciences of Science Learning: An Interdisciplinary Discussion, September 6, Washington, DC. Department of Psychology, Carnegie Mellon University.

Sirotnik, K.

1983 What you see is what you get: Consistency, persistence, and mediocrity in classrooms. *Harvard Educational Review*:53:16-31.

Sizer, T.

1992 *Horace's Compromise: The Dilemma of the American High School.* 3rd ed. Boston: Houghton Mifflin.

Slavin, R.E.

    1980   Effects of individual learning expectations on student achievement. *Journal of Educational Psychology* 72(4):520-24.

    1995   A model of effective instruction. *The Educational Forum* 59(Winter): 166-176.

Smith, M.S., and J. O'Day

    1991   Systemic school reform. In *The Politics of Curriculum and Testing*, S. Furhman and B. Malen, eds. Bristol, PA: Falmer Press.

Spiegel, D.L.

    1994   A portrait of parents of successful readers. *Fostering the Love of Reading: The Affective Domain in Reading Education.* Newark, DE: International Reading Association.

Steele, C.M.

    1992   Race and the schooling of black Americans. *Atlantic Monthly* 262(4):68-78.

    1997   A threat in the air: How stereotypes shape the intellectual identities and performance of women and African Americans. *American Psychologist* 52:613-629.

Steele, C.M., and J. Aronson

    1995   Stereotype threat and the intellectual test performance of African-Americans. *Journal of Personality and Social Psychology* 69:797-811.

Stevenson, H.W., and J.W. Stigler

    1992   *The Learning Gap: Why Our Schools Are Failing and What We Can Learn from Japanese and Chinese Education.* New York: Simon and Schuster.

Stigler, J., R. Shweder, and G. Herdt, eds.

    1989   *Cultural Psychology: The Chicago Symposia on Culture and Development.* New York: Cambridge University Press.

Stipek, D.J.

    1993   *Motivation to Learn: From Theory to Practice.* Boston, MA: Allyn and Bacon.

Stokes, D.E.

    1997   *Pasteur's Quadrant: Basic Science and Technological Innovation.* Washington, DC: Brookings Institution Press.

Strauss, C., and N. Quinn

    1997   *A Cognitive Theory of Cultural Meaning.* Cambridge and New York: Cambridge University Press.

Stroup, A.L., and L.N. Robins

    1972   Elementary school predictors of high school dropouts among black males. *Sociology of Education* 45(2):212-212.

Suchman, L.

    1987   *Plans and Situated Actions: The Problem of Human-Machine Communication.* Cambridge and New York: Cambridge University Press.

Tobin, J.J., D. Wu, and D. Davidson

    1989   *Preschool in Three Cultures: China, Japan and the United States.* New Haven: Yale University Press.

Treisman, P.U.

    1996   Enabling Broader Access to Algebraic Understanding. Paper prepared for the Committee on Developments in the Science of Learning for the Sciences of Science Learning: An Interdisciplinary Discussion. Dana Center for Mathematics and Science Education, University of Texas.

Turnbull, B.J., H. McCollum, M.B. Haslam, and K. Colopy
   1994   *Regional Educational Laboratories: Some Key Accomplishments and Limitations in the Program's Work.* Washington, DC: Policy Studies Associates.

Tyack, D., and L. Cuban
   1995   *Tinkering Toward Utopia: A Century of Public School Reform.* Cambridge, MA: Harvard University Press.

U.S. Department of Education
   1990   *A Profile of the American Eighth Grader: NELS:88 Student Descriptive Summary.* NCES 90-45-8. Washington, DC: U.S. Government Printing Office.
   1996   *Urban Schools: The Challenge of Location and Poverty.* NCES 96-184. Washington, DC: U.S. Government Printing Office.
   1997   *Digest of Education Statistics, 1997.* Washington, DC: U.S. Government Printing Office.
   1998   Office of Education Research and Improvement Draft Report. October.

Vosniadou, S., and W.F. Brewer
   1989   The Concept of the Earth's Shape: A Study of Conceptual Change in Childhood. Unpublished paper, Center for the Study of Reading, University of Illinois, Champaign.

Vygotsky, L.S.
   1978   *Mind in Society.* Cambridge, MA: Harvard University Press.

Webb, N., and T. Romberg
   1992   Implications of the NCTM Standards for mathematics assessment. In *Mathematics Assessment and Evaluation*, T. Romberg, ed. Albany, NY: State University of New York Press.

Weiss, C.H.
   1980   Knowledge creep and decision accretion. *Knowledge: Creation, Diffusion, and Utilization* 1(3):381-404.
   1987   Evaluating social programs: What have we learned. *Society* 25(1) 40-45.
   1991   Policy research: Data, ideas, or arguments. Pp. 307-332 in *Social Sciences and Modern States: National Experiences and Theoretical Crossroads.* P. Wagner, C.H. Weiss, B. Wittrock, and H. Wollmann, eds. Cambridge: Cambridge University Press.
   1995   The haphazard connection: Social science and public policy. *International Journal of Education Research* 23(2):137-150.
   1998a Improving the use of evaluations: Whose job is it anyway? *Advances in Educational Productivity* 7:263-276.
   1998b Have we learned anything new about the use of evaluation? *American Journal of Evaluation* 19:21-33.

Wertsch, J.
   1991   *Voices of the Mind.* Cambridge, MA: Harvard University Press.

Wertsch, J., G.D. McNamee, J.B. McLane, and N. Budwig
   1980   The adult-child dyad as a problem-solving system. *Child Development* 51:1215-1221.

Wilson, K.G., and C.K. Barsky
   1998   Applied research and development: Support for continuing improvement in education. *Daedalus* 127(4):233-258.

ORDER CARD
(Customers in North America Only)

Improving Student Learning

Use this card to order additional copies of **Improving Student Learning**. All orders must be prepaid. Please add $4.50 for shipping and handling for the first copy ordered and $0.95 for each additional copy. If you live in CA, DC, FL, MD, MO, TX, or Canada, add applicable sales tax or GST. Prices apply only in the United States, Canada, and Mexico and are subject to change without notice.

___ I am enclosing a U.S. check or money order.

___ Please charge my VISA/MasterCard/American Express account.

     Number:

_____

PLEASE SEND ME: **6489**

Qty.	Code	Title	Price
___	SERP	**Improving Student Learning**	
		single copy	$12.95
		2-9 copies	$10.50
		10 or more copies	$ 8.95

Subtotal	_____	
Shipping	_____	
Tax	_____	

Please print.   **Total** _____

Name _____

Address _____

City _____ State _____ Zip Code _____

FOUR EASY WAYS TO ORDER

- **Electronically:** Order from our secure website at: **www.nap.edu**
- **By phone:** Call toll-free 1-800-624-6242 or (202) 334-3313 or call your favorite bookstore.
- **By fax:** Copy the order card and fax to (202) 334-2451.
- **By mail:** Return this card with your payment to NATIONAL ACADEMY PRESS, 2101 Constitution Avenue, NW, Lockbox 285, Washington, DC 20055.

To be eligible for a discount, all copies must be shipped and billed to one address.

ORDER CARD
(Customers in North America Only)

Improving Student Learning

Use this card to order additional copies of **Improving Student Learning**. All orders must be prepaid. Please add $4.50 for shipping and handling for the first copy ordered and $0.95 for each additional copy. If you live in CA, DC, FL, MD, MO, TX, or Canada, add applicable sales tax or GST. Prices apply only in the United States, Canada, and Mexico and are subject to change without notice.

___ I am enclosing a U.S. check or money order.

___ Please charge my VISA/MasterCard/American Express account.

     Number:

_____

PLEASE SEND ME: **6489**

Qty.	Code	Title	Price
___	SERP	**Improving Student Learning**	
		single copy	$12.95
		2-9 copies	$10.50
		10 or more copies	$ 8.95

Subtotal	_____	
Shipping	_____	
Tax	_____	

Please print.   **Total** _____

Name _____

Address _____

City _____ State _____ Zip Code _____

FOUR EASY WAYS TO ORDER

- **Electronically:** Order from our secure website at: **www.nap.edu**
- **By phone:** Call toll-free 1-800-624-6242 or (202) 334-3313 or call your favorite bookstore.
- **By fax:** Copy the order card and fax to (202) 334-2451.
- **By mail:** Return this card with your payment to NATIONAL ACADEMY PRESS, 2101 Constitution Avenue, NW, Lockbox 285, Washington, DC 20055.

To be eligible for a discount, all copies must be shipped and billed to one address.

National Academy Press
Leading the World in Science, Technology, and Health

Visit our website at

www.nap.edu

Use the form on the reverse of this card to order additional copies

or visit our website.

National Academy Press
Leading the World in Science, Technology, and Health

Visit our website at

www.nap.edu